Crafting an ANGEL a Day

Edited by Laura Scott

HOUSE of
WHITE
BIRCHES

Crafting an Angel a Day

Editor: Laura Scott
Design Manager: Vicki Blizzard
Technical Editor: Läna Schurb
Copy Editor: Mary Nowak
Publications Coordinator: Tanya Turner

Photography: Tammy Christian, Jeff Chilcote, Jennifer Fourman
Photography Stylist: Arlou Wittwer
Photography Assistant: Linda Quinlan

Production Coordinator: Brenda Gallmeyer
Book Design: Dan Kraner
Cover Design: Vicki Macy
Production Artist: Vicki Macy
Angel Illustrations: Annie Lang
Production Assistants: Shirley Blalock, Marj Morgan
Traffic Coordinator: Sandra Beres
Graphs/Drawings: Leslie Brandt, Allison Rothe, Jessica Rothe

Publishers: Carl H. Muselman, Arthur K. Muselman
Chief Executive Officer: John Robinson
Marketing Director: Scott Moss
Marketing Manager: Craig Scott
Product Development Director: Vivian Rothe
Publishing Services Manager: Brenda R. Wendling

Printed in the United States of America
First Printing: 2000
Library of Congress Number: 99-95549
ISBN: 1-882138-55-4

An Angel a Day ANYONE?

Dear Crafters,

Over the course of human history, men and women have found comfort and strength in believing we are protected and helped every day by angels. The Bible even says angels are "ministering spirits sent forth to serve those who will inherit salvation."

In recent years, angels have become a very popular crafting character and home decorative accent. Although the angels we craft vary greatly in appearance, we still find strength and inspiration in them.

In this collection of more than 100 delightful angels to craft, you'll find many different styles and themes of angels. From sweet teddy bear angels and heartwarming snow angels, to elegant Victorian angels and adorable holiday angels, you'll find dozens of ideas for gifts and decorations to share with all your craft-loving family and friends.

We've also included an entire chapter of occupational angel projects which make perfect gifts for those many people—teachers, doctors, nurses and more—who make our day-to-day lives go more smoothly.

So be sure to share this collection of engaging angels with everyone you love! In doing so, you'll give them a little bit of handcrafted heaven!

CRAFTS FOR SALE!

We hope you enjoy crafting and sharing each of these angels with friends and family for many years.

Warm regards,

Laura Scott

Laura Scott, Editor
Crafting an Angel a Day

CONTENTS

Country ANGELS

Teddy Bear ANGELS

Victorian ANGELS

Snow ANGELS

Career ANGELS

my teacher is a blessing

With their warm eyes, huggable bodies and sweet personalities, teddy bears have worked their way into all our hearts! This collection of teddy bear angel crafts is sure to warm your heart and home as you craft and share each project!

Teddy Bear ANGELS

T his sweet T-shirt is sure to become your little girl's (and your) favorite! She'll want to wear it day in and day out!

"Bless My Little Heart" T-Shirt

Design by Annie Lang

Materials

- ♥ White 50/50 cotton/polyester blend T-shirt (see Project Notes)
- ♥ So-Soft fabric acrylic paint from DecoArt:
  White #DSS1
  Raspberry pink #DSS8
  Baby blue #DSS16
  Terra cotta #DSS22
  Dark chocolate #DSS23
  Black #DSS24
  Flesh tan #DSS35
- ♥ Shimmering Pearls fabric paints from DecoArt:
  Golden yellow #DSP2
  Ultra blue #DSP22
  White #DSM1 So-Soft Metallic fabric paint from DecoArt
- ♥ Paintbrushes:
  ½" angle shader
  #4 flat scrubber
  #1 liner
  #4 pointed round
  #4 round scrubber
- ♥ T-shirt painting board (see Project Notes)
- ♥ Rubber bands or pins

Project Notes

A child's T-shirt size 2–4 (XS) was used for sample. Use a photocopier to enlarge or reduce pattern as desired to fit any size T-shirt or other item (tote bag, jacket, sweat pants, etc.).

Pattern may be transferred to shirt with a fabric transfer pencil, graphite or some other transfer method, if desired. Refer to General Instructions on page 188.

Before painting, launder T-shirt without using fabric softener to remove sizing; let dry completely and press with a warm iron as needed to remove wrinkles.

T-shirt painting board should be large enough to hold shirt taut without overstretching the fabric. A stiff piece of cardboard covered with plastic wrap or a plastic bag may be substituted.

Instructions

1. Insert T-shirt painting board in T-shirt and secure with rubber bands or pins so front of shirt is smooth and secure, but not overstretched.

2. Referring to pattern (page 36), paint wings, skirt, headband and right section of heart with white acrylic paint. Fill in underside areas of skirt near hemline with baby blue. While white paint is still wet, load pointed tip of shader with a touch of baby blue and apply color around edges of these areas to create shading; also shade "pleat" lines in skirt and "gathers" in wings and headband. Let dry.

3. Add shine by painting over areas painted in step 2 with white metallic paint. Using liner, paint a band of golden yellow along bottom of skirt about ¼" from hemline.

4. Paint muzzle flesh tan; while still wet, shade muzzle with a touch of terra cotta applied near edge of heart.

5. Paint remaining sections of bear with terra cotta, blending in a touch of raspberry pink on bear's cheeks; while still wet, shade all edges and inner ears with a touch of dark chocolate applied with shader.

6. Paint heart on bear's foot with raspberry pink.

7. In upper left portion of heart, paint background around moon shapes with ultra blue; let dry. Fill in moons with golden yellow. Add random dots around moons with wooden tip of paintbrush handle dipped in golden yellow.

8. In bottom portion of heart, paint background around star shapes with baby blue; let dry. Fill in stars with golden yellow. Add random dots with brush handle and golden yellow as in step 7.

9. Using liner and ultra blue, paint tiny starbursts over metallic white background in right-hand section of heart. When dry, add random dots with brush handle and golden yellow as in step 7.

10. Using liner throughout and black paint, add eyes, nose, facial details and all other outlining and details. Using white acrylic, dot tiny highlight onto each cheek; thin a tiny amount of white acrylic with water and add a "comma" stroke of thinned mixture to highlight right side of nose.

11. Using round brush and ultra blue, paint lettering. As desired, apply random baby blue dots around bear and lettering with tip of paintbrush handle. ✳

Patterns on page 36

W ith his bright red bow and festive holly wreath, this huggable felt ornament will add holiday cheer to your Christmas tree!

Felt Teddy Angel Ornament

Design by Chris Malone

Materials
- Felt:
  9" x 12" sheet tan
  9" x 12" sheet white
  1½" x 8" strip red
  3" square deep green
  Scrap of light green
  Scrap of off-white
- Coordinating 6-strand embroidery floss: brown, tan, off-white, red, deep green and light green
- Embroidery needle
- Pompoms:
- 7mm brown
- 5 (5mm) red
- 2 (5mm) half-round beads
- Brown acrylic paint
- Small paintbrush
- 8" piece brown pearl cotton
- Polyester fiberfill
- Craft glue

Project Notes
Use 2 strands embroidery floss and Blanket Stitch for all sewing unless instructed otherwise.

Lay felt pieces together wrong sides facing when joining body, wings and wreath pieces.

Instructions
1. Referring to patterns (page 37), cut pieces from felt: two bodies and two ears from tan, two sets of wings from white, one bow from red, two wreaths from deep green, 10 holly leaves from light green, and one snout from off-white.

2. Sew around each ear with brown floss. Pin snout to one body and sew in place with off-white; sew one ½" brown Straight Stitch down snout from top edge. Pin body halves together; sew together with brown floss, stuffing lightly as you stitch and catching ears in top of head.

3. Pin wings together; sew together with tan floss (do not stuff). Using same floss, sew a Running Stitch down center between wings; pull floss to gather tightly; knot floss and clip ends. Applying glue along gathering stitch, glue wings to back of bear.

4. Blanket Stitch all around edges of

bow with red floss. Fold ends of bow to center, matching narrow areas. Wrap red floss around center of bow to hold in place; glue bow to bear's neck.

5. Pin wreaths together; sew together around center opening with light green floss. Stuffing wreath lightly, sew around outer edge.

6. Referring to stitch diagram (page 37), sew two deep green Fly Stitches on each holly leaf. Arrange leaves on front of wreath; applying a narrow bead of glue down center of back of each leaf, press leaves in place. Glue red pompoms to wreath for holly berries. Glue wreath to one of bear's hands.

7. Paint half-round beads brown; let dry. Glue beads to bear's face for eyes. Glue brown pompom to top of snout for nose.

8. Sew hanging loop of brown pearl cotton through top of teddy bear's head. ✳

Patterns on page 37

Make a dozen of these cheery ornaments to give to family, friends and co-workers this Christmas!

Angel Bear Wreath Ornament

Design by Jackie Haskell

Materials

- Sculpey III modeling compound:
  Black #042
  Chocolate #053
  Tan #301
  Dusty rose #303
  Emerald #323
  Ivory brilliant #501
  Red #582
- 2 black seed beads
- Straight-edge tool for cutting and adding details
- Straight pin
- Round wooden toothpick
- Small piece of 24-gauge gold-tone wire
- 2" piece of metallic gold chenille stem
- Craft glue
- Oven-proof plate
- Oven

Project Notes

Refer to photo throughout.

Soften and work modeling compound with your fingers until it is pliable before shaping and sculpting. Clean your hands thoroughly when changing colors to avoid mixing colors.

Instructions

1. Cut a quarter-section from emerald compound brick; roll it into a ball, then roll back and forth on clean work surface to make a 12" rope. Fold rope in half and twist halves together. Trim both ends and press ends together to make a wreath.

2. Cut a quarter-section from chocolate compound; cut off ⅛ of this small piece for teddy bear's body. Roll into a ball, then shape into a 1" teardrop.

3. Roll two pea-size balls of chocolate compound; cut ¼ from each ball and set aside to use for ears. Form the remaining ¾ pieces into identical cones for front legs. Attach smaller ends of cones to body; flatten and round larger ends for paws.

4. Lay wreath so that seam is at center top. Place teddy bear's body and front legs on wreath; body will curve slightly around wreath.

5. For head, cut another ⅛ from original quarter-section of chocolate compound. Roll it into a ball, then shape in a rounded teardrop.

6. Referring to Fig. 1, push two seed beads on their sides into head for eyes; press until none of the bead hole shows. Using straight pin, indent two eyelashes for each eye.

Fig. 1

7. Roll a pea-size ball of tan compound; cut ⅛ from ball and press into a small disk for bear's muzzle. Press onto bottom half of head; indent a single vertical line with straight edge. Roll a tiny, tiny ball from black compound and press onto muzzle at top of line for bear's nose. Press head onto body.

8. For ears, roll each small piece of chocolate compound reserved in step 3 into a ball and flatten slightly. Using straight edge, add straight detail lines to ears; attach ears to head.

9. Using toothpick, make a hole in top of head at center back for inserting halo later.

10. Roll two pea-size balls of chocolate compound for back legs. Form each into ½"-long log; flatten one end and attach to body; form other end into a foot. Attach back legs to body.

11. Roll pea-size ball of dusty rose. Cut off ⅛ of ball, and cut that small piece in half; flatten each piece into a tiny disk and attach to bottoms of feet for foot pads.

12. For wings, roll two pea-size pieces of ivory compound; flatten each into a teardrop shape and add detail lines with straight edge. Press wings onto back of body.

13. For berries on wreath, roll a pea-size ball of red compound and cut into 16 pieces. Roll 15 into tiny balls and attach to wreath in five groups of three.

14. Bend a small piece of wire into a ½"-long U-shape; press ends into top of wreath, leaving loop for hanging.

15. Bake ornament on oven-proof plate in preheated 275-degree oven for 10 minutes. Cool completely.

16. For halo, bend gold chenille stem around pencil to make loop; leave a straight ¼" stem to insert in hole in bear's head; clip off excess and bend halo over. ✸

H ere's a delightful project that looks like a quilt but requires no more than a few embellishing stitches!

"Bee an Angel" Wall Hanging

Design by Chris Malone

Materials

- ❤ Fabrics:
  ⅓ yard natural osnaburg
  ¼ yard red-and-black mini check
  ½ yard blue check or plaid
  Scrap of white-and-tan print
  Scraps of mottled brown
  Scraps of denim-like blue
  Scrap of gold print
  Scrap of black solid
- ❤ Fusible webbing
- ❤ Embroidery hoop
- ❤ Embroidery needle
- ❤ Low-loft craft or quilt batting
- ❤ 6-strand embroidery floss: black and red
- ❤ Quilting threads: ecru, red and blue
- ❤ Hand-sewing needle
- ❤ Quilting needle (optional)
- ❤ Sewing machine (optional)
- ❤ Air- or water-soluble fabric marking pen
- ❤ Seam sealant
- ❤ Buttons:
  2 (½") red flat
  2 (⅜") black flat
  ⅜" black shank
- ❤ Metal snips or wire cutters
- ❤ 2 (5mm) black half-round beads
- ❤ Wooden products:
  ⅞" wooden "split wren" half-egg
  ¾"-wide wooden heart cutout
  2 (1¼") wooden half-balls
  15" (½"-wide) wooden slat
- ❤ Acrylic paints: gold, black and white
- ❤ Small paintbrush
- ❤ Walnut stain
- ❤ Satin-finish varnish
- ❤ Fine-point black permanent marking pen
- ❤ 2 (1") sawtooth hangers
- ❤ Hot-glue gun
- ❤ Iron

Project Notes

All piecing is done right sides facing.

All measurements include ¼" seam allowance.

Border strips are cut long and trimmed later to allow for individual differences in piecing.

Complete all embroidery with 2 strands embroidery floss.

Let all paints and stain dry before applying additional paint or varnish.

Center Panel

1. With pencil, mark 9" x 11" rectangle on osnaburg. Cut out approximately 1" outside marked lines.

2. Referring to pattern (page 38) and using air-soluble pen, write "bee an angel" and trace curved line for bee's trail onto osnaburg.

3. Place osnaburg in embroidery hoop. Using black floss, Backstitch letters and make French Knots at ends of letters as shown.

4. Trace all appliqué pieces onto paper side of fusible web; cut out, cutting just outside traced lines. Referring to manufacturer's instructions, iron web onto wrong sides of fabrics: overalls on blue denim, wings on white-and-tan print, teddy bear pieces on mottled brown, beehive onto gold print and hive opening onto black fabric. Cut out appliqués on traced lines; remove paper backing. Arrange pieces on osnaburg and iron in place.

5. Using black floss, stitch bee's path with Running Stitch; Backstitch straight line down from bear's left paw to top of hive. Add bow at top of hive with two Lazy Daisy Stitches and two Straight Stitches. Add single ⅝" Straight Stitch down bear's face to define nose/mouth.

6. For overalls pocket, cut 1" square denim-like fabric; apply seam sealant to edges and let dry. Using red floss and Running Stitch, sew pocket by hand to front of overalls, leaving top open.

Borders & Assembly

1. Trim osnaburg to marked 9" x 11" rectangle.

2. For inner border, cut 1" x 44" strip red-and-black checked fabric. Sew a border strip to each side of center panel; trim edges even. Sew a border strip to top and bottom; trim even. If one strip is not enough for all four sides, measure last side and cut strip to size.

3. Cut two 2½" x 30" strips from blue check fabric; sew to red-and-black border strips in the same manner. Press all seams outward.

4. Lay batting on flat surface; smooth out any bumps. Lay remaining piece of blue fabric right side up on top of batting for backing. Lay pieced top right side down on top of backing fabric. Pin through all layers to secure. Cut out backing and batting even with top.

5. Using matching blue thread, sew around all edges by hand or machine, leaving 5" opening at center bottom for turning. Trim batting close to seam and trim corners. Turn right side out and press. Fold in seam allowance along opening; Whipstitch closed.

6. With straight pins or basting stitch, secure all layers through centers of both borders. Using matching quilting thread and stitching by hand or machine, "stitch in the ditch" (as close to seam as possible) between center block and red-and-black border, and again between red-and-black and blue borders.

7. For hanging loops, cut two 4" x 6 ½" rectangles from red-and-black check. Fold each in half lengthwise, right sides facing, and sew along cut edges, leaving 2"

opening for turning. Clip corners and turn strips right side out; Whipstitch openings closed. Fold each loop over top of wall hanging, overlapping top about 1¼" on front and back and positioning loops about 2" in from sides. Secure loops to hanging by sewing through all loops with black thread, attaching black flat button to front of loop as you sew.

Finishing

1. For hanky, cut 1" square from red-and-black fabric; apply seam sealant to edges and let dry. Fold hanky in half diagonally, then fold pointed sides to back and tuck hanky into overalls pocket so point peeks out from top; secure hanky with a dab of glue.

2. For nose, snap shank off black button with snips; glue to face. Glue half-round beads in place for eyes.

Sew red buttons to overalls with red thread, sewing through fabric layers.

3. Paint half-egg and half-balls gold on all surfaces. Paint black stripes on half-egg to resemble bee; add a tiny white dot at narrow end of egg (bee's head) for eye. Paint heart cutout white on all surfaces for bee's wings. Stain wooden slat with walnut stain.

4. Coat all painted and stained pieces with satin varnish.

5. Draw dashed line around edge of bee's wings (heart) with marking pen. Glue pointed end of wings to back of bee; glue bee to wall hanging at end of stitched "path."

6. Attach sawtooth hanger to back of slat at each end. Glue painted half-ball to each end of slat on front. Slip hanging loops onto slat. ✳

Patterns on page 38

Fig. 1

Sew this adorable stuffed bear angel to either dress up a corner of your home or as a special gift for your little one!

Bearly an Angel

Design by Veleta Stafney

Materials

- 3 pairs boy's white tube socks, shoe size 3–11½
- 4 (¾") white flat buttons
- ⅝" wooden mushroom button
- 2 (9mm) black half-round eyes
- ¾ yard (1½"-wide) burgundy floral ribbon
- 1 pair 6"-wide gold puffy angel wings from Darice
- 3" grapevine wreath
- Acrylic paints: peach and white
- Paintbrush
- Air- or water-soluble fabric marker
- Polyester fiberfill
- Hand-sewing needle
- 5" doll-sculpting needle
- White carpet thread
- White sewing thread
- Stylus or toothpick
- Needle-nose pliers
- Pink powdered cosmetic blusher
- Cotton-tip swab
- Fabric glue

Project Notes

Use sewing thread unless instructed otherwise.

Because of the glued-on button eyes and nose, project should not be used as a toy for children under age 3. For youngsters of this age, complete sculpting as instructed, but substitute Satin Stitched eyes and nose, or flat pieces of felt securely sewn in place.

Instructions

1. *Body:* Cut cuff from one sock; discard cuff. Turn sock wrong side out; stuff firmly. Sew gathering stitch along raw edge; pull gathers tight and knot.

2. *Head:* Cut 4½" from cuff of one sock and discard cuff portion. Turn sock wrong side out and stuff firmly. Sew gathering stitch along raw edge; pull gathers tight and knot. With fabric-marking pen, mark dot for position of nose 2¼" below toe seam.

3. *Sculpting face:* Thread doll needle with carpet thread; knot ends together. Insert needle from back of head straight through dot marking nose, wrapping thread around center of gathered edge. Repeat, pulling thread tight to indent cheeks. Knot thread at back of head.

4. *Ears:* Using fabric-marking pen and referring to Fig. 1 (above), mark position of ears. Sew gathering stitch in a line from A to B on left side, going through both layers of sock and stuffing. Knot thread at back of ear. Repeat on right side for other ear.

5. *Facial features:* For nose, paint mushroom button peach; let dry. Glue nose to face at nose dot marked in step 2. For each eye, thread doll needle with carpet thread. Insert needle from back of head at nose indent, coming out at front ½" above nose. Insert needle ⅛" to left; pass needle back through head to nose indent; repeat. Pull thread to indent area for left eye; knot thread at back of head. Repeat for right eye, inserting needle ⅛" to right of point ½" above nose. Snap off stems of eyes with pliers; glue one eye into each indentation.

6. Pin head to top of body; glue or stitch by hand to secure.

7. *Legs:* Cut cuff from one sock and discard cuff. Turn sock wrong side out and stuff firmly. Sew gathering stitch along raw edge; pull gathers tight and knot. With fabric-marking pen, mark a dot 1½" from toe seam. Thread doll needle with carpet thread; insert needle through dot coming out on opposite side of leg. Insert needle ⅛" over and back through leg; repeat. Pull thread to indent leg and knot thread at back of leg. Repeat for other leg.

8. *Arms:* Cut 4" from cuff edge of one sock; discard cuff section. Finish arms as for legs, making indentation 1" from toe seam.

9. *Attaching legs:* Thread doll needle with an extra-long strand of carpet thread; knot ends together. Insert needle 1" from bottom of body through one side of body to other side, then through one leg, through one hole in a white button, back through other buttonhole, back through same leg and back through body. Then pass needle through second leg, through one hole in a second white button, and through another hole in button. Repeat twice, passing threaded needle through buttons, legs and body, pulling thread tight. Insert needle a final time through button and leg, bringing needle and thread out between leg and body; knot thread.

10. *Attaching arms:* Repeat step 9, attaching arms 1" from neck.

11. Apply cosmetic blusher to cheeks and inner ears with cotton-tipped swab. Using stylus, add highlight dots of white paint to cheeks and white comma stroke to nose. Tie ribbon around neck in a bow; trim ribbon tails at an angle. Glue wings to back of body. Separate strands of grapevine wreath; sew or glue one spiral to head for halo. ✽

You'll have fun making this sweet-as-can-be ornament with rusty tin, acrylic paints, wooden hearts, a scrap of lace and tiny artificial flowers!

Li'l Teddy Ornament

Design by Bonnie Stephens

Materials

- ♥ Aleene's Premium-Coat acrylic paints:
  Dusty blush #OC 111
  Black #OC 176
  Ivory #OC 179
  Yellow ochre #OC 184
  Burnt umber #OC 185
- ♥ Aleene's Enhancers satin finish #EN 102
- ♥ Paintbrushes:
  ¾" flat
  10/0 liner
- ♥ Tin pieces from D&CC:
  4" Rusty Tin heart with holes
  2 (2⅛") Rusty Tin-tiques folk hearts
- ♥ 2 (½") wooden heart cutouts from Woodworks Inc.
- ♥ 4" piece (1¾"- to 2"-wide) ecru filet crochet, lace or eyelet
- ♥ Matching ecru thread or floss
- ♥ 3 small dried, silk millinery flowers
- ♥ Thick tacky craft glue
- ♥ 8" piece 20-gauge wire
- ♥ Paper towels
- ♥ Needle-nose pliers

Project Notes

Paint only one side of tin pieces.
Let paints dry between coats.

Painting

1. Using flat paintbrush and dusty blush paint, paint one side and all edges of each wooden heart.

2. Apply a little ivory paint to flat paintbrush; brush on paper towel until very little paint remains, then paint smaller tin hearts with nearly dry brush.

3. Using flat paintbrush, base-coat larger heart with yellow ochre.

4. Referring to photo and pattern for face (page 45), paint muzzle area with ivory paint which has been mixed with a small amount of yellow ochre.

5. Using handle of liner brush dipped in black paint, dot on two eyes. Thin a small amount of black paint with a little water; using liner brush, paint on nose and mouth as shown.

6. Using flat brush, shade around muzzle, tops of ears, inner ears and top of head with burnt umber.

7. Using liner brush and ivory, add highlight dots in upper right portion of both eyes and wooden hearts; add highlight line on right side of nose.

Assembly & Finishing

1. Glue wooden hearts to teddy bear's face for cheeks. Glue smaller tin hearts to wrong side of bear's face to form wings. Let dry.

2. Using flat brush, apply one or two coats of satin finish to all surfaces.

3. Gather lace by tying it in the center with matching thread; glue to bottom of larger tin heart. Glue small flowers to center of lace "bow."

4. For hanger, insert wire ends through holes in larger tin heart from back to front; twist kinks and coils in ends of wire with needle-nose pliers to hold hanger in place. ✷

Pattern on page 45

G
ive two gifts in one by tucking this year's gift for Mom or Sis in this delightful tote bag!

Tangled-Up Tote

Design by Kathy Wegner

Materials

- ❤ 9¾" x 11¼" natural canvas tote bag
- ❤ Scribbles 3-D paints from Duncan Enterprises:
  Shiny butterscotch #SC 113
  Shiny tea #SC 166
  Glittering gold #SC 302
- ❤ Tulip gunmetal #65080 pearl fabric paint from Duncan Enterprises
- ❤ Tulip paint extender #65123 from Duncan Enterprises
- ❤ #3 round scrubber stiff paintbrush
- ❤ 8 (1") tree lights from Dress It Up Jack Frost #364 buttons-and-charms packet by Jesse James & Co.
- ❤ Fine-point black permanent fabric marker
- ❤ Black sewing thread and hand-sewing needle
- ❤ Cardboard cut to fit inside tote bag and covered with plastic wrap, or paper towels

Instructions

1. Insert plastic-covered cardboard into tote bag so front surface lies flat (or stuff bag with paper towels to keep paint from bleeding through to other side).

2. Referring to pattern (page 39), draw pattern on front of tote bag with fine-point black fabric marker.

3. Mix a small amount of shiny butterscotch paint with an equal amount of paint extender; paint teddy bear except for feet bottoms, muzzle and wings with paint mixture. Clean brush.

4. Mix a small amount of shiny tea paint with an equal amount of paint extender; paint teddy bear's muzzle and feet bottoms with mixture. Clean brush.

5. Paint around inside of wing sections with glittering gold paint. Let paints dry completely.

6. Redraw any lines as needed with fabric marker; let dry.

7. Add string for lights with gunmetal fabric paint; let dry. Sew lights along light string with needle and thread as shown. ✳

Pattern on page 39

F

rame a favorite photograph of your little angel in this delightful photo frame! It makes a great gift for Grandma, too!

Heavenly Bear Frame

Design by Kathy Wegner

Materials
- 5" x 7" papier-mâché photo frame with 4½" x 3" oval opening
- Aleene's Premium-Coat acrylic paints:
  Light blue #OC 149
  Dusty blue #OC 153
  White #OC 173
- Craft foam: white and tan
- Fine-point black permanent marking pen
- Matte-finish spray varnish
- Small foam paintbrush
- Small piece of natural sponge
- Paper towels
- Thick tacky craft glue

Project Note
Refer to photo throughout.

Painting Frame
1. Remove plastic protector from frame, if one is included. Using foam brush, paint entire frame on all surfaces with two coats light blue, letting paint dry between coats.

2. Wet natural sponge with water; squeeze dry. Dip sponge into dusty blue; blot sponge on paper towels until almost no paint remains on sponge. Dab sponge lightly on frame where you want to position clouds. Rinse sponge in water and squeeze dry.

3. Dip sponge into white; blot once or twice onto paper towel, then dab on frame over dusty blue areas, leaving some dusty blue visible to give depth and dimension to clouds. Let dry.

4. Lightly sponge a bit more white onto clouds, especially along their lower edges. Let dry.

5. Spray frame with varnish; let dry.

Teddy Bear
1. Referring to patterns (page 39), cut one teddy bear head and two paws from tan craft foam and one pair of wings from white.

2. Using fine-point black marking pen, add bear's facial features, define toes on paws, and add details to wings.

3. Glue wings to back of frame; glue teddy bear's head and paws to front of frame; let dry. Insert plastic photo protector and photo in frame. ✳

Patterns on page 39

I f you enjoy adding just a hint of holiday cheer to your outfit, then this darling angel is just right for you!

Teddy Angel Pin

Design by Paula Bales

Materials

- ♥ 4" round ecru doily
- ♥ 1" wooden knob
- ♥ Acrylic paints: chocolate brown and pink-mauve
- ♥ Slick paints: black and white
- ♥ Paintbrushes:
  Small all-purpose paintbrush
  Stencil brush
- ♥ Muslin scraps
- ♥ Fine-point black permanent marking pen
- ♥ 20-gauge wire
- ♥ Brown loopy doll hair
- ♥ Pink-mauve ⅛"-wide satin ribbon
- ♥ Paper towels
- ♥ Hot-glue gun
- ♥ 1" pin back
- ♥ Hand-sewing needle and ecru sewing thread (optional)

Project Notes

Refer to photo throughout.

Let all paints dry between coats.

Use all-purpose paintbrush unless instructed otherwise.

Instructions

1. Paint knob on all surfaces with chocolate brown paint.

2. Referring to pattern (above), cut two ears from muslin; paint each chocolate brown; let dry thoroughly.

Glue ears to back of head (see photo).

3. Dab stencil brush in pink-mauve paint; pounce most of paint off onto folded paper towels; referring to Fig. 1, use nearly dry brush to pounce pink-mauve cheeks onto knob on areas indicated by diagonal lines. Repeat to color centers of ears.

Fig. 1

4. Paint nose pink-mauve. Dot on eyes with black slick paint. Add highlight dot to each eye with white slick paint.

Ear
Cut 2
from
muslin

5. Using fine-point marking pen, add mouth line, eyebrows and details at corners of eyes.

6. Bend wire into a 1" circle; twist ends together. Glue straight stem to back of bear's head; bend circle to front for halo. Glue a tuft of loopy hair between ears.

7. Fold doily in half for wings; glue bear's head to center with folded edge of doily at top. Glue or sew pin back to back of doily wings.

8. Tie ribbon in small bow; trim ends. Glue bow below bear's "chin." ✳

A ngel collectors will adore this darling keepsake box which reads, "Old Teddy Bears Go to Heaven."

Teddy Bear Heaven Box

Design by Barbara Woolley

Materials

- ♥ 10" x 8" x 5" oval papier-mâché box with lid
- ♥ 5 (2") wooden knobs
- ♥ Imitation snow paste
- ♥ Ceramcoat acrylic paints from Delta Technical Coatings Inc.:
  - Pale yellow #2005
  - Tangerine #2043
  - Lavender #2047
  - Dark brown #2053
  - Empire gold #2412
  - Antique rose #2469
  - White #2505
  - Black #2506
  - Opaque blue #2508
  - Opaque yellow #2509
  - Blue lagoon #2528
  - Caribbean blue #2530
  - Silver pine #2534
- ♥ Paintbrushes
- ♥ Sea sponge
- ♥ Metallic marking pens: 18K gold and silver
- ♥ Paint pens in desired colors (optional; see Project Notes)
- ♥ Fine-point black permanent marking pen
- ♥ Matte-finish exterior/interior varnish
- ♥ Multipurpose craft cement

Teddy Bear Heaven Box Stars

Project Notes

Refer to photo throughout for placement and color suggestions.

Let paints, pens, ink and varnish dry between coats.

Paint pens in desired colors can be substituted for some of the paint colors; paint pens make it very simple to embellish teddy bears' gowns and stars with colorful details.

Box

1. Using blue lagoon, base-coat interior of box and lid and bottom exterior of box.

2. Base-coat lid exterior with a combination of opaque blue and blue lagoon, applying darker color at edge and blending into lighter color in center.

3. Base-coat exterior box sides with a combination of opaque blue, white and blue lagoon, applying darker color at edges and blending into lighter color in middle.

4. Base-coat knobs with opaque blue.

5. Add stripes to painted knobs with metallic silver marking pen. Cement four knobs to bottom of box for feet; cement remaining knob to center of lid for handle.

Lettering & Angel Bears

1. Using metallic silver marking pen, write "Old Teddy Bears Go to Heaven" around top of lid; shade letters with black marking pen as desired.

2. Referring to patterns (pages 40 and 41), trace bears evenly spaced around sides of box; add stars randomly to box sides and lid.

3. Following manufacturer's instructions, apply imitation snow paste to teddy bear angels' wings; let dry.

4. Referring to photo throughout, paint teddy bear angels and stars:

Bears—Paint dark brown; blend dark brown with a bit of pale yellow and/or white to create a lighter shade for painting muzzles and highlighting. Paint eyes with black, and add white highlights.

Gowns—Base colors are Caribbean blue, antique rose, lavender and silver pine; embellish with stripes, dots, checks and other details in different colors (paints or paint markers) and in silver and gold.

Stars—Base-coat with opaque yellow, then highlight with other colors (paints or paint markers), gold and silver.

5. Add details—fur, whiskers and other details on bears and gowns—with fine-point marking pen.

6. Give each angel bear a halo with gold metallic marking pen.

7. Using sea sponge and white paint, sponge clouds over blue background on box and lid.

8. Apply two coats of varnish to box and lid, inside and out.

Patterns on page 40

F

Fabric paints and fusible web make this sweet T-shirt-and-barrette set a snap to make, and a delight to wear and share!

Little Angel Bear Outfit

Design by June Fiechter

Materials
- ♥ Light blue cotton/polyester blend T-shirt (see Project Notes)
- ♥ Washable fabrics:
  8½" x 6½" and 4½" x 2¼" pieces pink
  8½" x 6½" and 2½" x 3¼" pieces white
  8½" x 4½" and 2" x 2½" pieces brown
- ♥ Iron-on adhesive:
  2 (8½" x 6½") pieces
  8½" x 4½" piece
- ♥ Scribbles dimensional fabric paints from Duncan Enterprises:
  Crystal Gel pink lemonade
  Iridescent white mist #SC 201
  Shiny black #SC 139
- ♥ Crafter's acrylic paints from DecoArt:
  Sandstone #DCA14
  Dusty mauve #DCA25
- ♥ Fabric medium
- ♥ Paintbrushes
- ♥ 2" barrette
- ♥ Hot-glue gun
- ♥ Iron
- ♥ Pressing cloth
- ♥ T-shirt painting board (see Project Notes)
- ♥ Rubber bands or pins

Project Notes
A child's long-sleeved T-shirt, size 10–12 (medium), was used for sample.

Before painting, launder T-shirt and fabrics without using fabric softener to remove sizing; let dry completely and press with a warm iron as needed to remove wrinkles.

T-shirt painting board should be large enough to hold shirt taut without overstretching the fabric. A stiff piece of cardboard covered with plastic wrap or a plastic bag may be substituted.

Pink fabric used on sample has woven-in pattern, and some sections are highlighted with brushed-on pink lemonade paint. If your fabric has no pattern, highlight sections of wings with pink lemonade paint as desired to add depth.

Instructions
1. Following manufacturer's instructions, fuse 8½" x 6½" pieces of iron-on adhesive to wrong sides of matching pieces of pink and white fabric; fuse 8½" x 4½" piece adhesive to wrong side of matching piece of brown fabric.

2. Referring to patterns (pages 42 and 43), trace wings for both T-shirt and barrette on paper backing on pink fabric. In same manner, trace both clouds on back of white fabric, and all teddy bear pieces on back of brown fabric. Cut out; separate pieces for T-shirt from those for barrette.

T-Shirt
1. Peel paper backing from larger cloud and wings. Referring to manufacturer's instructions, iron pieces onto front of T-shirt. (Pieces fit together like a puzzle without overlapping.)

2. Mix sandstone paint with fabric medium according to instructions on medium bottle. Using mixture, paint oval snout on bear's face; paint inner ears, and add details to paws to define "toes." Let dry.

3. Using same paint/medium mixture, outline head and both paws to keep fabric edges from raveling; let dry.

4. Mix dusty mauve paint with fabric medium; paint bear's cheeks with mixture. Let dry.

5. Peel backing from painted teddy bear pieces and position on shirt; protect painted fabric with a pressing cloth and iron pieces in place. Let shirt cool.

6. Insert T-shirt painting board in shirt and secure with rubber bands or pins so front of shirt is smooth and secure, but not overstretched. Using crystal gel pink lemonade paint, paint portions of wings as desired (see Project Notes) and outline wings; paint halo. Using iridescent white mist paint, outline cloud; draw several stars on light blue background of shirt. Using shiny black paint, add triangular nose and round eyes. Let shirt dry flat for 24 hours before wearing.

7. Follow recommendations on paint bottles for laundering.

Barrette
1. Peel paper backing from smaller cloud. Referring to manufacturer's instructions, fuse cloud adhesive side down onto wrong side of 3¼" x 2½" piece white fabric; trim away excess backing fabric. Repeat with wings and teddy bear pieces, using smaller pieces of pink and brown fabrics.

2. Repeat steps 2–4 as for T-shirt.

3. Hot-glue barrette high on wrong side of clouds; hot-glue wings on top of clouds. Hot-glue teddy bear head, then paws over wings and cloud. Let glue dry and cool completely.

4. Add outlines and details with crystal gel pink lemonade, iridescent white mist and shiny black dimensional paints as for T-shirt in step 6. Let dry for 24 hours before wearing. ✶

Patterns on page 42

Country Teddy Face
Cut 2 ears from craft foam

D

ress up the door to your country home with this sweet woodcraft. Buttons, fabric patches and wooden hearts add to this little lady's charm!

Country Teddy Door Decor

Design by Bonnie Stephens

Materials
- Aleene's Premium-Coat acrylic paints:
  Deep mauve #OC 104
  Dusty blue #OC 153
  Black #OC 176
  Ivory #OC 179
  Yellow ochre #OC 184
  Burnt umber #OC 185
- Aleene's oak stain #AW 302
- Aleene's Enhancers:
  Satin finish #EN 102
  All-purpose primer #EN 104
- Paintbrushes:
  ¾" flat
  #12 flat
  10/0 liner
  Spatter brush
- Stylus
- Walnut Hollow Victorian angel
- 2" square of light-colored craft foam
- Wooden products:
  2 (¼") buttons
  2 (½") buttons
  2 (1") heart cutouts
  1¼" heart cutout
- 6" piece (1"-wide) ecru filet crochet, lace or eyelet
- 4" x 6" piece country-style fabric in small print, plaid or check
- Coordinating sewing thread and hand-sewing needle
- Small fabric scraps
- 6" piece jute twine
- Thick tacky craft glue
- 20-gauge wire
- Fine sandpaper
- Paper towels
- Craft drill with small bit
- Needle-nose pliers

Project Notes
Let primer and paints dry between coats.

Fabric on sample is a country-style checked pattern in tan and barn red.

Painting
1. Using ¾" flat paintbrush, apply primer to all wooden pieces; sand.

2. Referring to pattern throughout, cut two ears only from craft foam.

3. Using ¾" flat paintbrush, base-coat foam ears, head and two 1" heart cutouts with yellow ochre. Base-coat body and wings with ivory. Sand.

4. Combine ivory with a little yellow ochre; base-coat muzzle with mixture using #12 flat brush. Thin a little black paint with water; using 10/0 liner brush, paint mouth, nose and footpads on yellow ochre heart cutouts (feet); paint dashed line around edges of wings and body. Dip stylus in black paint; dot on eyes.

5. Using #12 flat brush and burnt umber, shade muzzle and inner ears.

6. Using oak stain thinned with a little water, antique bear's body and wings, wiping thinned stain on with a paper towel and immediately wiping it off.

7. Using thinned black paint, spatter ivory wings and body very lightly.

8. Coat bear with one or two coats of satin finish.

9. Using #12 flat brush, paint remaining heart cutout deep mauve; sand lightly to give it a distressed look. Paint one ½" button deep mauve and the other dusty blue; paint one ¼" button dusty blue and the other yellow ochre.

Assembly & Finishing
1. Glue ears to front of head as shown. Tie jute twine in tiny bow and glue between ears.

2. With needle and thread, gather fabric along one long edge. Glue to bear along gathered edge for apron. Glue lace across top edge of apron for apron band.

3. Glue yellow ochre button atop deep mauve heart; glue heart to bear below mouth. Glue larger dusty blue button below heart. Just below hem of apron, down center of legs, glue smaller dusty blue button, then deep mauve button. Glue yellow ochre hearts to bottom of bear for feet, points up.

4. Cut three small patches from fabric; glue to wings. With thinned black paint and 10/0 liner, add stitching lines at corners of patches.

5. For hanger, drill small hole near top of each wing, about 2" in from ends. Insert wire ends through holes from back to front; twist kinks and coils in ends of wire with needle-nose pliers to hold hanger in place. ✳

E

ither of these bright and colorful projects, including a tin-punch door hanger and painted gift bag, would make a great gift! Or make both and tuck the door hanger inside the gift bag!

Mama Bear Angel Gifts

Designs by Sandra Graham Smith

Materials
Door Hanger
- Tracing paper
- 7" x 8" piece aluminum flashing
- Tin snips
- Masking tape
- Finishing nails
- Larger nail
- Hammer
- Pressed-wood board
- Silver star garland

Gift Bag
- 8" x 10" brown paper gift bag with handles
- 1 sheet red tissue

Both Projects
- Enamel paints: white, red, green, brown, pink
- Metallic gold glitter paint
- Small paintbrush
- Fine-point marking pens: black and white
- 1 sheet white card stock
- Large snowflake paper punch
- Tacky craft glue

Door Hanger
1. Trace pattern (page 44) onto tracing paper; cut out. Trace around pattern onto aluminum; cut out with tin snips.

2. Tape paper pattern to aluminum with masking tape. Place on pressed-wood board.

3. Punch design using finishing nail and hammer, moving from dot to dot and changing nails when point dulls. Using larger nail, punch large holes for hanger in tops of wings where indicated.

4. Remove pattern and tape; turn punched tin over. Rough side will be right side.

5. Referring to photo and pattern for color placement, apply paint inside punched lines with thick strokes. Allow to dry completely.

6. Paint two small white circles on bear's face for eyes; let dry completely.

7. Using black marker, draw eyes, nose and mouth; add stitch lines and pleats on collar and apron.

8. Using white marker, draw snowflakes on green portions of bear's clothing.

9. Punch snowflake from card stock; glue between hands.

10. Thread silver star garland through larger holes in wings for hanger; twist ends to secure.

Gift Bag
1. Referring to pattern (page 44), transfer design onto gift bag. (Disregard dots for punching.)

2. Repeat steps 5–8 from Door Hanger instructions.

3. Punch 10 snowflakes from card stock; glue one between hands and remainder to surface of gift bag.

4. Stuff red tissue into bag. ✳

Pattern on page 44

Dress up your refrigerator and keep yourself organized by crafting this handy refrigerator magnet. It's large enough to hold up your long Christmas list!

Teddy Angel Magnet

Design by Paula Bales

Materials

- Metal end from a refrigerated roll container
- Wooden circles: 1¼" and 2 (¾")
- Aerosol off-white metal primer
- Acrylic paints: chocolate brown and light beige
- Slick paints: black, white and red
- Paintbrushes: Small all-purpose paintbrush Stencil brush
- ¼" black pompom
- ⅛"-wide red satin ribbon
- White craft foam
- 20-gauge wire
- Fine-point black permanent marking pen
- Paper towels
- Hot-glue gun
- 3" piece adhesive-backed magnet

Project Notes

Refer to photo throughout.

Let all paints dry between coats.

Use all-purpose paintbrush unless instructed otherwise.

Instructions

1. Spray metal can end with primer. Using stencil brush, "pounce" chocolate brown paint on all surfaces of can end.

2. Referring to patterns (page 45), cut two ears and one set of wings from craft foam; paint ears chocolate brown and wings light beige; let dry thoroughly. Paint larger wooden circle light beige for snout; paint smaller circles chocolate brown for paws.

3. Dot outline of wings with fine-point marking pen; add random dots to surface of wings with red slick paint.

4. Glue snout to head, paws to bottom of head, ears to top back of head and assembled head to center of wings.

5. Dab stencil brush in red paint; pounce most of paint off onto folded paper towels; referring to Fig. 1, use nearly dry brush to pounce red cheeks onto snout on areas indicated by vertical lines.

6. Dot on eyes with black slick paint. Add highlight dot to each eye with white slick paint.

7. Using fine-point marking pen,

Fig. 1

add mouth, eyebrows and details at corners of eyes; outline paws, face and ears. Glue pompom to snout for nose.

8. Bend wire into a 2" circle; twist ends together. Glue straight stem to back of bear's head; bend circle to front for halo. Tie ribbon in a bow around base of halo.

9. Remove backing from magnet strip; press onto back of wings. ✳

Patterns on page 45

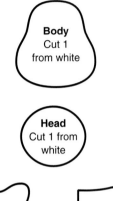

Base
Cut 1 from black

Body
Cut 1 from white

Head
Cut 1 from white

Hind Leg
Cut 2 from black

Front Leg
Cut 2 from black

Help your child craft one of these sweet pencil toppers for each of his or her friends!

Panda Pencil Angel

Design by Jackie Haskell

Materials
- Craft foam: white and black
- 2 (5mm) round black wiggly eyes
- 2" piece iridescent pink twisted paper cord
- 2" piece iridescent chenille stem
- ¾"-wide bow tied from ⅛"-wide mauve satin ribbon
- Pink powdered cosmetic blusher
- Cotton-tip swab
- ¼" round paper punch
- Black ultra-fine–point permanent marking pen
- Craft glue
- Hot-glue gun
- Pencil

Project Note
Glue pieces together with hot-glue gun unless instructed otherwise.

Instructions
1. Referring to patterns, cut head and body from white craft foam; cut legs and base from black craft foam. Using paper punch, punch one white circle for panda's snout and two black circles for ears.

2. Roll base into a tube which will slide over eraser end of pencil and stay in place; glue overlapping edges together.

3. Position base seam at center front and, referring to photo throughout, glue body onto base, concealing seam, so that bottom edges of body and base are even.

4. Glue edges of bottom legs to body; glue edges of top legs to base where base and body meet.

5. Using craft glue, glue eyes to head; with cotton-tip swab, apply blusher to panda's cheeks.

6. Glue snout to panda's head; draw round nose and mouth line with marking pen. Glue ears to top of head, edge to edge.

7. For wings, untwist paper cord and smooth it out; trim so it measures 1¼" wide. Twist this piece twice in the center. Glue wings to back of base.

8. For halo, wrap chenille stem around pencil; twist ends to make halo stem and cut off excess so stem measures ½". Glue stem to back of head and bend halo over top of head. Glue halo stem into hole. Glue ribbon bow to panda. ✳

Not only is this craft cute as a button, but it is also made from recycled materials such as a tuna can, old ribbon and more!

Plant Poke Teddy Angel

Design by Paula Bales

Materials

- Clean, empty 10-ounce tuna can, one end removed
- Metal end from a refrigerated roll container
- Drill with ¼" and ³⁄₁₆" bits
- Aerosol off-white metal primer
- Acrylic paints: chocolate brown, light beige and red
- Slick paints: black and white
- Paintbrushes:
  Small all-purpose paintbrush
  Stencil brush
- ½" wooden knob
- Muslin scraps
- 20-gauge wire
- Fine-point black permanent marking pen
- Brown loopy doll hair
- 18" (¼") wooden dowel
- 3" piece red-and-white gingham wired paper ribbon or recycled ribbon
- Paper towels
- Hot-glue gun

Project Notes

Refer to photo throughout.

Let all paints dry between coats.

Use all-purpose paintbrush unless instructed otherwise.

Preparation & Painting

1. Scrape any dried glue from outside of can. Drill ¼" hole in center of one side of can for dowel; drill a ³⁄₁₆" hole opposite it on other side for inserting halo.

2. Spray can inside and out with two coats of primer. Spray metal end of roll can with primer also.

3. Paint tuna can inside and out with two coats chocolate brown paint; paint metal end of roll can with light beige. Paint wooden knob with black slick paint.

4. Referring to pattern (page 44), cut two ears from muslin; paint each chocolate brown; let dry thoroughly.

Assembly & Finishing

1. Referring to photo, glue beige can end to brown tuna can for snout (hole for dowel should be centered below snout).

2. Dab stencil brush in red paint; pounce most of paint off onto folded paper towels, then pounce red cheeks on beige and brown portions of teddy bear's face with nearly dry brush. Repeat to color centers of ears.

3. Referring to Fig. 1 (page 44), glue black knob nose to bear's face; dot on black eyes with black slick paint. Add highlight dot to each eye with white slick paint.

4. Using fine-point marking pen, add mouth line, eyebrows and details at corners of eyes.

5. Bend wire into a 3" circle; twist ends together. Insert straight stem into top of bear's head; bend circle to front for halo; secure stem of halo with glue.

6. Glue ears to bear's head; glue a tuft of loopy hair between ears, concealing base of halo.

7. Glue end of dowel in larger hole.

8. Tie ribbon in bow around dowel as shown; notch ribbon ends. ✳

Patterns on page 44

Wish peace and goodwill to all your friends and family who visit your home during the holidays with this colorful quilt!

Angel of Peace Quilt

Design by Angie Wilhite

Materials

- Fabric:
  - ⅓ yard gold print for interior square
  - ¼ yard blue print for border
  - ½ yard muslin for backing
  - 2 (5") squares cream fabric for star
  - Remnants of green, blue, light gold and tan solids or prints for appliqués
- 2" square black felt
- Deep gold double-fold ½" bias tape
- Products from Pellon:
  - ⅓ yard Wonder Under fusible transfer web
  - ⅛ yard heavy-duty Wonder Under fusible transfer web
  - ⅓ yard Sof-Shape fusible interfacing
  - 5" square fusible fleece
  - ½ yard Stitch-n-Tear fabric stabilizer
  - ½ yard quilter's fleece
- Coats Dual Duty Plus rayon embroidery floss to match green, blue and light gold appliqué fabrics
- All-purpose sewing threads to match green, blue and light gold appliqué fabrics, blue border fabric and bias tape
- White quilting thread
- Embroidery floss: black and red
- Sewing machine with satin stitch
- Hand-sewing needle
- 2 (⅛") black buttons
- Heart button #4258 La Mode Quilter's Folk Art button from Blumenthal Lansing Co.
- 2 (⅝") plastic rings
- Fabric glue
- Iron
- Fine-point black permanent fabric-marking pen

Project Notes

Refer to photo throughout.

Use photocopier with enlarging capabilities to enlarge pattern to 115 percent before cutting.

Follow manufacturer's instructions for applying fusible products to fabrics.

Quilt Top

1. Launder fabrics and muslin without using fabric softener; press with warm iron.

2. From gold print, cut one 11" square.

From blue print, cut two 2¼" x 11" strips and two 2¼" x 14" strips.

3. Using matching sewing thread and ¼" seam allowance, center 11" blue strips along top and bottom of gold square, right sides facing; sew in place and press seam allowance to outside. Center 14" blue strips on sides of gold square; sew in place. Press quilt top so it lies flat.

4. Fuse heavy-duty transfer web to wrong side of one cream fabric square; fuse fleece to wrong side of

other cream square. Peel backing from both pieces; press adhesive sides together. Referring to patterns (page 46) throughout, cut star from fused cream fabric.

5. Apply interfacing, then transfer web to wrong sides of green, blue, light gold and tan appliqué fabrics. Trace pieces for bear onto paper side of tan fabric; trace wings onto paper side of light gold; trace "land" portions of background globe onto paper side of green fabric; trace "water" onto blue. Cut out appliqués.

6. Apply heavy-duty transfer web to back of black felt; trace nose onto paper side and cut out.

7. Position pieces for globe in center of gold block; peel off paper backing and fuse. Add wings, teddy bear and nose; fuse.

8. Pin or baste fabric stabilizer to back of block. Using matching rayon floss for top thread and all-purpose thread in bobbin, Satin Stitch around wings and globe, beginning stitching on appliqués that appear to be at back of design. Remove fabric stabilizer; trim thread ends.

9. Using 2 strands black embroidery floss throughout, Blanket Stitch around teddy bear pieces; sew buttons to face for eyes. Using red floss, sew heart button to teddy bear's chest.

10. Using 2 strands black embroidery floss, blanket-stitch around edges of star. Write "Peace" on star with fine-point marking pen. Glue star to quilt.

Assembly

1. Cut 18" square from muslin and another from quilter's fleece. Lay muslin right side down; top with fleece. Lay quilt top on fleece, right side up. Baste layers together.

2. Using white quilting thread, quilt around world ¼" from edge. Quilt in the ditch on seam lines.

3. Trim fleece and backing so edges are even. Bind with bias tape.

4. Sew plastic rings to top corners on back of quilt for hangers. ✳

Patterns on page 46

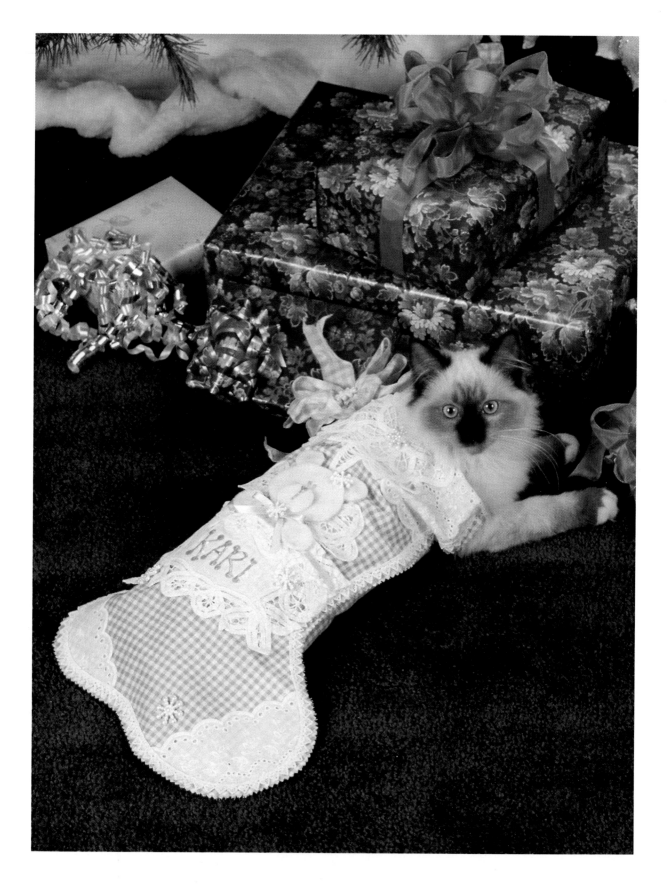

T his delicate, lacy delight is perfect for your little lady's very first Christmas. It looks just as charming in pale blue for a wee laddie or in any pastel. Fill it with nursery supplies for a spectacular shower gift!

Holiday Angel Christmas Stocking

Design by Cheryl Ball

Materials
- ¼ yard pink gingham-check fabric
- ½ yard scallop-edged 4¼"-wide white eyelet fabric
- 6" white rectangular Battenburg doily
- 6" oval white Battenburg doily
- 2 (2") white lace hearts
- 10" square ivory polar fleece fabric
- 2 yards (½"-wide) white lace trim
- 2 yards (1"-wide) wire-edge pink-and-white gingham ribbon
- 1 yard (¼"-wide) pink satin ribbon
- Assorted pearly white snowflake buttons or other white buttons
- Thick tacky craft glue
- Tulip bubble gum #65170 pearl dimensional fabric paint from Duncan Enterprises
- Tracing paper
- Pink powdered cosmetic blusher
- Cotton-tipped swab
- Pinking shears
- White sewing thread
- Sewing machine
- Iron

Pattern Note
Refer to photo throughout for placement of fabric pieces and painted details.

Stocking
1. Referring to stocking pattern (page 47), enlarge pattern to 175 percent and cut pattern from paper. Fold gingham fabric in half, wrong sides facing; lay paper pattern on top and pin to fabric through both layers. Cut out stocking halves with pinking shears. Remove paper pattern.

2. Using sewing machine and white thread, stitch stocking halves together, wrong sides facing, stitching ½" from cut edges and leaving top open.

3. Cut scallop-edged eyelet to fit across top of stocking between stitch lines; position eyelet so about ½" extends above stocking. Fold top ½" under to inside of stocking; press. Glue eyelet in place on front and inside stocking.

4. Cut additional pieces of eyelet to fit within stitch lines at heel and toe; glue in place.

5. Glue ½" lace trim over stitch line around front of stocking, folding ends over top of stocking to inside and gluing them down.

6. Glue oval doily lengthwise to center top of stocking over eyelet, folding any excess to inside; secure with glue.

Teddy Bear & Trim
1. *Use 6" rectangular Battenburg doily to make a "pocket" on front of stocking:* Lay doily flat and fold 1½" along one long side to front; this will be "cuff" at top of pocket. Press. Lay pressed doily on stocking as shown; glue pocket to stocking around sides and bottom.

2. Glue a length of pink satin ribbon across folded-over top of pocket, taking care not to glue pocket closed.

3. Referring to patterns (page 47), cut one large circle for head, three small circles for paws and muzzle, and two ears from ivory fleece fabric.

4. Apply powdered blusher to insides of ears and to cheek area on large fleece circle (teddy bear's head). Glue ears to back of head; glue one small fleece circle to head for muzzle.

5. Arrange heart-shaped doilies behind teddy bear's head to look like wings; bottoms of wings and teddy bear's head should be even with top of pocket. Glue teddy bear and wings to stocking.

6. Add a little blush to bottom edges of remaining small fleece circles for paws; glue paws, blushed edge down, to top of pocket cuff, taking care not to glue pocket closed.

7. Tie a bow from remaining pink satin ribbon; glue to cuff between paws; glue snowflake atop bow. Glue all but one of the remaining snowflakes or buttons to stocking as desired.

8. Tie multilooped bow from wire-edge ribbon; tack to upper left corner of stocking. Glue one last snowflake or button to center of bow.

9. Using bubble gum paint, dot on eyes and nostrils; draw line on bear's muzzle. Write baby's name on center of doily pocket, adding dots of paint at ends of letters; let dry completely. ✳

Patterns on page 47

Treat overnight guests to a bed decorated with delightful felt-appliqué pillow toppers and cuddly blanket!

Country Angel Pillowcase and Blanket

Designs by Angie Wilhite

Materials
Each Project
💜 ¼ yard creamy white #J8X Rainbow Shaggy Plush Felt from Kunin Felt

💜 Felt scraps: black and white

💜 Coordinating fabric remnants: gold, green, tan and blue

💜 Black 6-strand embroidery floss

💜 Cranberry sewing thread

💜 Hand-sewing needle

💜 3 (⅜") flat cranberry buttons

💜 Iron

Each Pillowcase
💜 Dark cranberry plaid dish towel from Wimpole Street Creations

💜 Sewing machine (optional)

💜 ⅓ yard HeatnBond Lite iron-on adhesive from Therm O Web

💜 ⅓ yard pressing paper

Blanket
💜 44" x 64" cranberry fleece blanket

💜 ⅔ yard HeatnBond Lite iron-on adhesive from Therm O Web

💜 ⅔ yard pressing paper

Project Notes
Refer to photo throughout.

Patterns (page 48) are for pillowcase; for blanket, use photocopier with enlarging capabilities to enlarge patterns to 125 percent before cutting.

Pillowcase
1. Launder towel and all fabrics without using fabric softener; press with warm iron (press shaggy plush felt from wrong side). Fold dish towel in half lengthwise; set aside.

2. Following manufacturer's instructions, fuse iron-on adhesive to wrong side of felt and fabrics. Referring to patterns (page 48), trace pieces onto paper backing: trace teddy bear pupils and nose onto black felt, and whites of eyes onto white felt; trace all other teddy bear pieces onto creamy white shaggy plush felt; trace tree and three hearts onto green fabric and trunk onto tan; trace wings onto gold fabric and three stars onto blue.

3. Cut out all traced pieces; peel off paper backing.

4. Position felt and fabric appliqué pieces on center front of folded dish towel. Cover design with pressing paper; fuse in place.

5. Using 2 strands black embroidery floss, Blanket Stitch around all design pieces. With cranberry thread, sew button to center of each green fabric heart.

6. Fold dish towel in half lengthwise, wrong sides facing. Using ¼" seam allowance, sew pillowcase together along long edge and one short end. Leave remaining short end open for inserting pillow. Turn pillowcase right side out.

Blanket
1. Launder blanket and all fabrics without using fabric softener; press with warm iron (press shaggy plush felt from wrong side).

2. Repeat steps 2–5 as for pillowcase, positioning design in one corner of blanket as shown. ✳

Patterns on page 48

Bless My

Little Heart!

Felt Teddy Angel Ornament

Continued from page 10

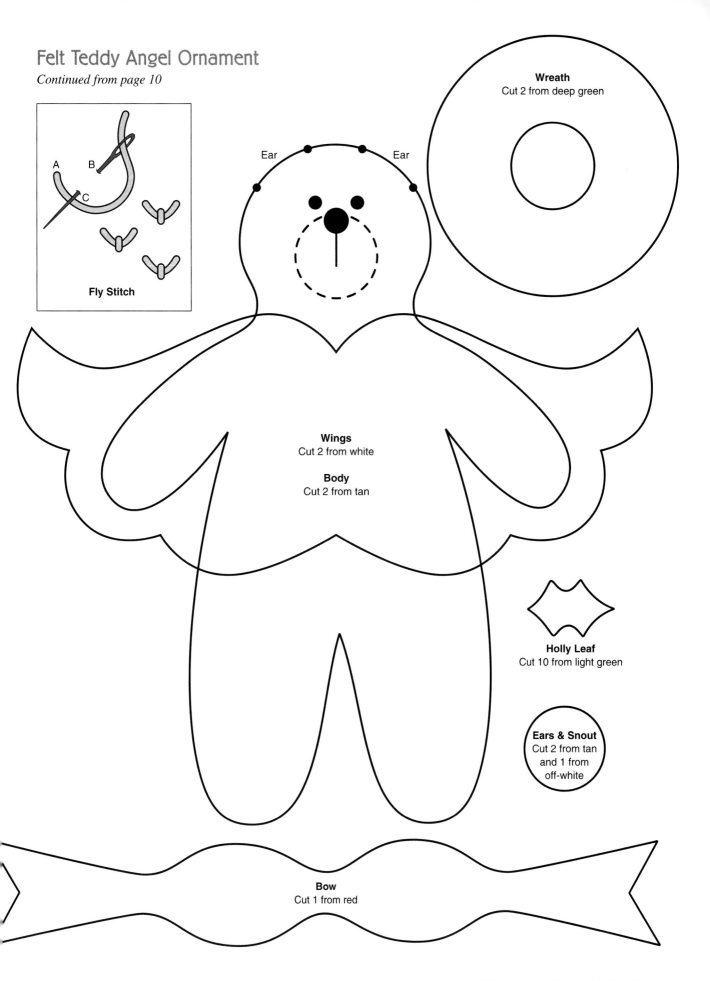

Fly Stitch

Ear   Ear

Wreath
Cut 2 from deep green

Wings
Cut 2 from white

Body
Cut 2 from tan

Holly Leaf
Cut 10 from light green

Ears & Snout
Cut 2 from tan
and 1 from
off-white

Bow
Cut 1 from red

Brown

White/Tan Print

Brown

Blue Denim

Gold Print   Black

bee
an
ange

Tangled-Up Tote

Continued from page 17

Tangled-Up Tote

Heavenly Bear Frame

Continued from page 18

Paw
Cut 2 from
tan foam

Wings
Cut 1 from white foam

Teddy Bear
Cut 1 from tan foam

Heaven Box Angel Bear A

Heaven Box Angel Bear B

Teddy Bear Heaven Box

Heaven Box Angel Bear C

Heaven Box Angel Bear D

T-Shirt Bear Face
Cut 1 from brown

Barrette Bear Face
Cut 1 from brown

T-Shirt Cloud
Cut 1 from white

Barrette Cloud
Cut 1 from white

Little Angel Bear Outfit

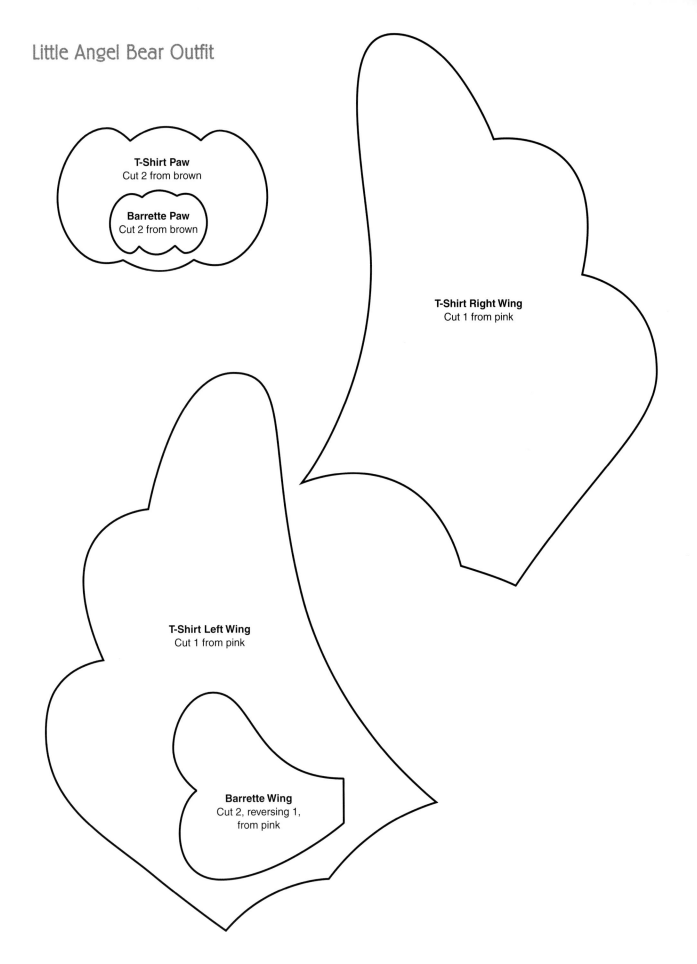

T-Shirt Paw
Cut 2 from brown

Barrette Paw
Cut 2 from brown

T-Shirt Right Wing
Cut 1 from pink

T-Shirt Left Wing
Cut 1 from pink

Barrette Wing
Cut 2, reversing 1,
from pink

Mama Bear Angel Gifts
Continued from page 26

Pink

Brown

Metallic gold

White

White

White

Green

Red

Green

Brown

Red

Green

Brown

Mama Bear Angel Gifts

Plant Poke Teddy Angel
Continued from page 29

Teddy Ear
Cut 2 from muslin

Fold and glue to head

Fig. 1

Teddy Angel Magnet
Continued from page 27

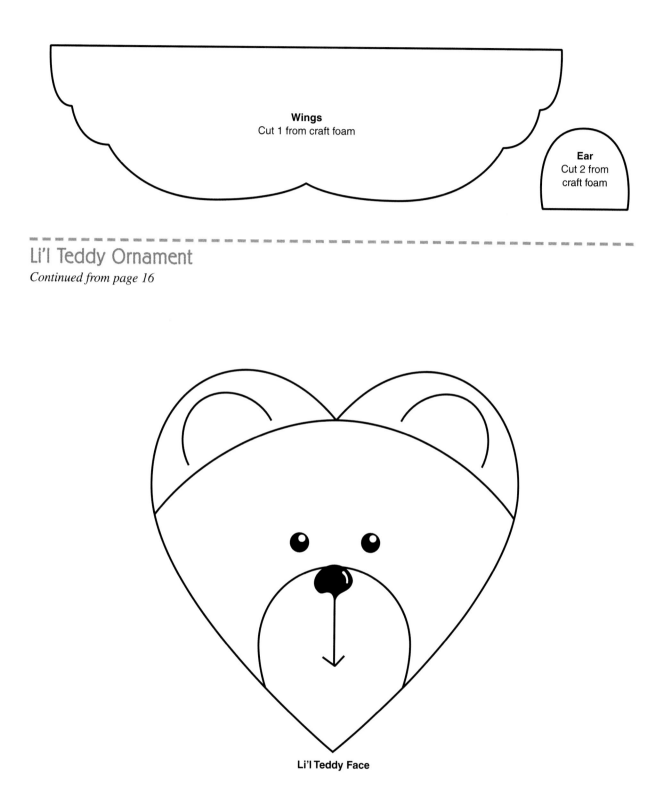

Wings
Cut 1 from craft foam

Ear
Cut 2 from craft foam

Li'l Teddy Ornament
Continued from page 16

Li'l Teddy Face

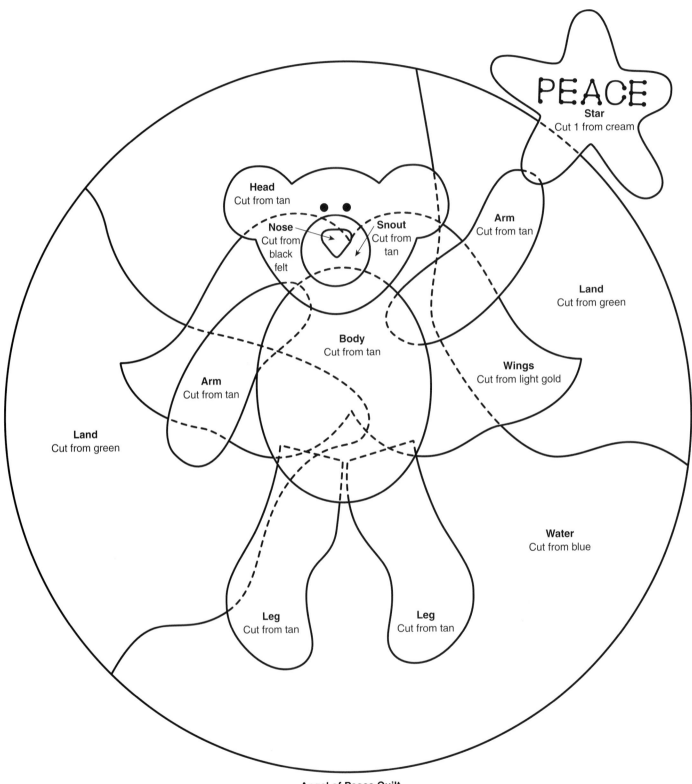

PEACE

Star
Cut 1 from cream

Head
Cut from tan

Nose
Cut from black felt

Snout
Cut from tan

Arm
Cut from tan

Land
Cut from green

Body
Cut from tan

Arm
Cut from tan

Wings
Cut from light gold

Land
Cut from green

Water
Cut from blue

Leg
Cut from tan

Leg
Cut from tan

Angel of Peace Quilt
Enlarge to 115% before cutting for full-size pattern

Continued from page 33

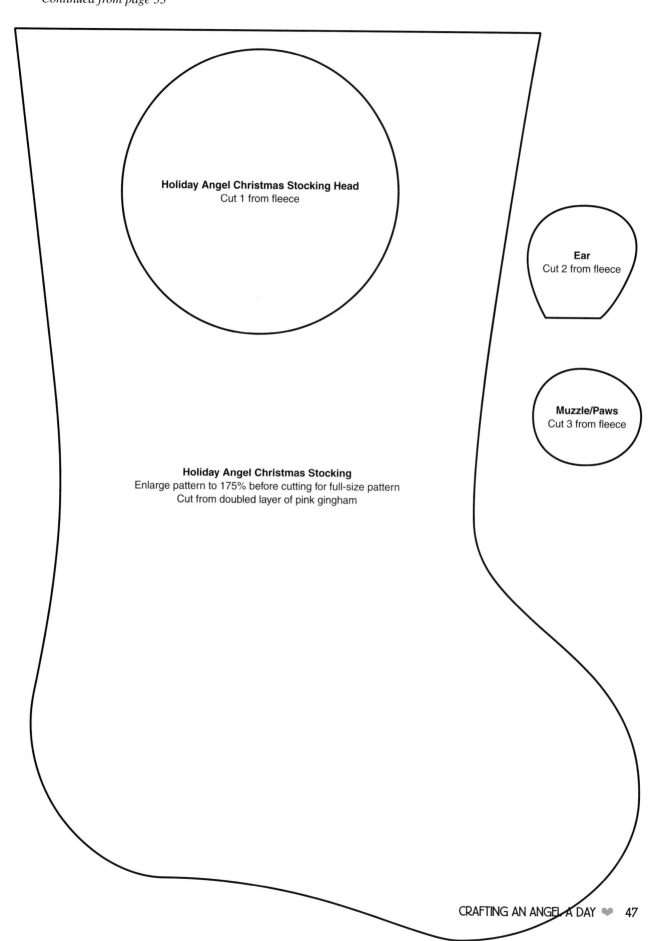

Holiday Angel Christmas Stocking Head
Cut 1 from fleece

Ear
Cut 2 from fleece

Muzzle/Paws
Cut 3 from fleece

Holiday Angel Christmas Stocking
Enlarge pattern to 175% before cutting for full-size pattern
Cut from doubled layer of pink gingham

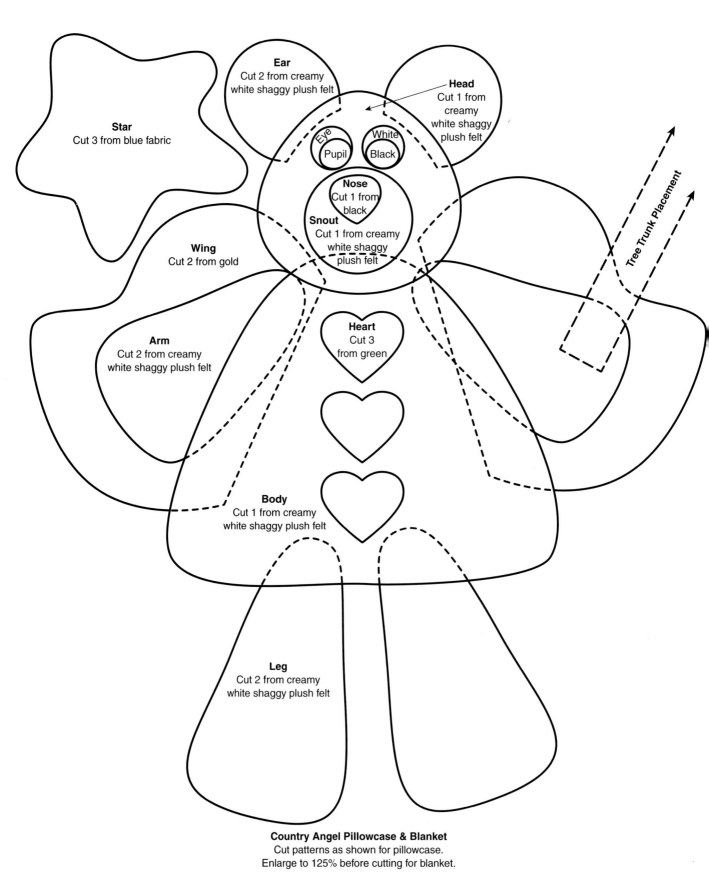

Star
Cut 3 from blue fabric

Ear
Cut 2 from creamy
white shaggy plush felt

Head
Cut 1 from
creamy
white shaggy
plush felt

Eye
Pupil

White
Black

Nose
Cut 1 from
black

Snout
Cut 1 from creamy
white shaggy
plush felt

Wing
Cut 2 from gold

Arm
Cut 2 from creamy
white shaggy plush felt

Heart
Cut 3
from green

Tree Trunk Placement

Body
Cut 1 from creamy
white shaggy plush felt

Leg
Cut 2 from creamy
white shaggy plush felt

Country Angel Pillowcase & Blanket
Cut patterns as shown for pillowcase.
Enlarge to 125% before cutting for blanket.

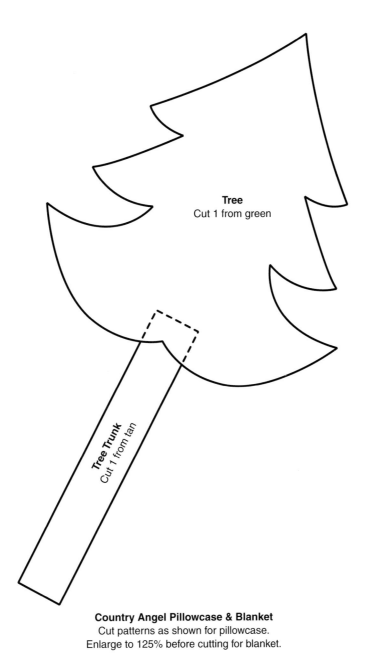

Tree
Cut 1 from green

Tree Trunk
Cut 1 from tan

Country Angel Pillowcase & Blanket
Cut patterns as shown for pillowcase.
Enlarge to 125% before cutting for blanket.

CRAFTS FOR SALE!

Crafters will be delighted with this warm and friendly collection of sweet country angels bursting with heavenly charm!

Country ANGELS

Light this special candle on Christmas Eve to bring in the holiday season of peace, love and goodwill to all!

Angel Prayers Candle Set

Design by Vicki Schreiner

Materials

- ♥ Star candle plate #17256 from Walnut Hollow
- ♥ 3" x 6" green pillar candle
- ♥ Ceramcoat metal primer #07-010 from Delta Technical Coatings
- ♥ Ceramcoat Sparkle Glaze #07-012 from Delta Technical Coatings
- ♥ Ceramcoat matte interior spray varnish #07-203 from Delta Technical Coatings
- ♥ Ceramcoat acrylic paints from Delta Technical Coatings:
  Brown velvet #2109
  Gypsy rose #2129
  Bouquet pink #2132
  Empire gold #2412
  Leprechaun #2422
  Bambi brown #2424
  Rose mist #2437
  Drizzle grey #2452
  Santa's flesh #2472
  Black cherry #2484
  White #2505
  Pine green #2526
  14K gold #2604
- ♥ Robert Simmons Expression paintbrushes from Daler-Rowney:
  ½" flat
  #6 filbert
  #6 round
  ¼" angle shader
  18/0 liner
  #0 liner
- ♥ Fine sandpaper
- ♥ Tack cloth
- ♥ White and black graphite papers
- ♥ Dull No. 2 pencil
- ♥ Ballpoint pen
- ♥ Paper towels
- ♥ Soft terry hand towel

Project Notes

Refer to photo throughout.

When base-coating is indicated, apply three coats of paint, allowing paint to dry between coats.

See General Instructions on page 188 for detailed directions for painting techniques including base-coating and shading.

Candle Preparation

1. Lightly buff candle surface with textured paper towel. Apply two coats metal primer using ½" flat brush, allowing primer to dry thoroughly between coats.

2. Touch prepared candle surface as little as possible. Instead of holding candle in your hand as you work, fold terry towel in half, place it on work surface, then lay candle on towel and use towel to roll candle as needed.

3. Copy pattern (page 84); lay on candle and hold in place (do not use tape). Slide white graphite paper under paper pattern, graphite side down. Trace main design using No. 2 pencil and light pressure. Do not transfer hash marks; these are for shading reference.

Candle Painting

1. Using #6 filbert brush or #6 round as needed to fit area, base-coat areas as follows: *wings*—white; *face and hands*—Santa's flesh; *dress*—bouquet pink; *patches*—black cherry.

2. Using black graphite paper, transfer details to dry base-coated design.

3. Shade as follows: *wings*—first with drizzle grey; let dry, then shade again along body with brown velvet; *face and hands*—lightly with Bambi brown; *dress*—first with rose mist; let dry, then shade again around arms with brown velvet.

4. Base-coat hair at this time using #6 round brush to apply empire gold in sweeping strokes toward face. Let dry. Double-load brush with brown velvet and empire gold and continue with sweeping strokes toward face; let dry. Shade around top of head with brown velvet.

5. Using 18/0 liner brush, line as follows: *eyes, lashes, nose and eyebrows*—brown velvet; *around hands*—brown velvet; *crosshatching on pockets*—leprechaun; *stitching on patches*—brown velvet; *stitching on wings*—brown velvet.

6. Using #0 liner brush and 14K gold, line halo and background stars; add background dots.

7. Blush cheeks with gypsy rose by dipping #6 filbert into tiny amount of paint and stroking onto paper towel until dry, then pounce onto cheeks. Randomly dot freckles using 18/0 liner brush with Bambi brown.

8. Use #6 filbert to apply one coat of sparkle glaze onto wings.

Candle Plate

1. Sand plate with fine sandpaper

Continued on page 83

Spread a little Christmas cheer and joy with this holiday plaque bearing the timeless message, "Joy to the world!"

Angel's Joy Plaque

Design by Kathy Wegner

Materials
- 9 green Woodsies jumbo wooden craft sticks from Forster Inc.
- Wooden products from Lara's Crafts:
  2 (2½") folk-art trees
  ¾" x ⅛" primitive star
  Angel wings
- 2" x 1¾" x ³⁄₁₆" wooden folk-art angel from Darice Craftwood
- Aleene's Premium-Coat acrylic paints:
  True red #OC 103
  Deep green #OC 140
  White #OC 173
  Blush #OC 183
  Yellow ochre #OC 184
- Paintbrush
- Aleene's Enhancers matte varnish #EN 107
- Aleene's Platinum Bond 7800 industrial strength craft adhesive
- Fine-point permanent black marker (see Project Notes)
- 7" piece natural jute twine
- Thick tacky glue
- Waxed paper

Project Notes
Refer to photo throughout.

Let all glue, ink and paints dry before proceeding with next step.

Test marking pen with varnish on a scrap of wood to make sure varnish will not make marker run. Thinned black acrylic paint applied with a liner brush may be substituted for marker.

Instructions
1. With tacky glue, glue 7 craft sticks together side by side; glue another stick across top of sticks, and the last stick across bottom. Sandwich glued craft sticks between waxed paper and weight with a heavy book until dry.

2. Paint front and side surfaces of remaining wooden pieces as follows: *tree trunks and star*—yellow ochre; *angel wings and "snow" on craft sticks (just above top edge of bottom crosspiece)*—white; *angel's head, hands and feet*—blush; *trees*—deep green; *angel's gown*—true red.

3. Using marker, outline angel, wings and trees with dashed black line; write "Joy to the world" on craft-stick crosspieces.

4. Glue trees, wings, angel and star to craft-stick plaque with industrial-strength craft glue; let dry for 24 hours. Seal with one or two coats of matte varnish, letting varnish dry between coats and after final application.

5. For hanger, glue ends of jute to back of plaque with industrial-strength craft adhesive. ✳

Bright colors and a fanciful design make this switch plate perfect for a child's room— a whimsical reminder that guardian angels are on the job, even when the lights go out.

Angel Switch Plate

Design by Mary Ayres

Materials

- Wooden switch plate from Wang's International Inc.
- 2 wooden gingerbread women from Lara's Crafts
- Woodsies wooden cutouts from Forster Inc.:
  4 (1") hearts
  4 (⅞") stars
  1¼" star
- Americana acrylic paints from DecoArt:
  Antique gold #DA9
  Lemon yellow #DA11
  Orchid #DA33
  Country blue #DA41
  Salem blue #DA43
  Sable brown #DA61
  Flesh tone #DA78
  True red #DA129
  Light buttermilk #DA164
- Paintbrushes:
  #6 and #8 round bristle
  #3 soft round
  Liner
- Pencil
- Fine-point black permanent marking pen
- Tacky craft glue
- Paper towels

Project Notes

Refer to photo and pattern throughout.

Let all paints dry between coats and before applying adjacent colors.

See General Instructions on page 188 for detailed directions for painting techniques including base-coating, dry-brushing and rouging.

Instructions

1. For angels, lightly pencil lines on gingerbread women to separate hands and faces from dresses. Base-coat faces and hands with flesh tone; base-coat one dress with Salem blue and the other with orchid.

2. For wings, base-coat hearts with light buttermilk. Dry-brush edges of wings and angels with antique gold.

3. Lightly pencil eyes on angels. Rouge cheeks with true red. Using liner brush, paint hair streaks on Salem blue angel with sable brown; paint hair streaks on orchid angel with lemon yellow.

4. Using tip of paintbrush handle, "stamp" lemon yellow dots on Salem blue dress and true red dots on orchid dress.

5. Using marking pen, draw eyes and stitching lines on angels and wings. Glue two wings to back of each angel.

6. Base-coat stars with antique gold. Dry-brush edges with light buttermilk. Using marker, draw stitching lines around stars ⅛" from edge.

7. Base-coat switch plate with country blue. Dry-brush edges with antique gold. Using black marking pen, draw stitching line around flat edges of switch plate and around center opening ⅛" from edge.

8. Plan arrangement of angels and stars on switch plate; glue in place. Using marking pen, draw halos and random-size stitching lines radiating from center of each side of stars. ✳

Angel Switch Plate

D
ress up a papier-
mâché box for a
special gift
package with cherubic charm!

Angel
Heart Box

Design by Mary Ayres

Materials
- 6" x 6" x 3" heart-shaped papier-mâché box with lid
- 6" crocheted white heart-shaped doily
- Tea bag
- Paper towels
- Clean metal lid from 12-ounce can of frozen juice
- ⅜" round wooden plug
- Americana acrylic paints from DecoArt:
  - Country red #DA18
  - Hi-lite flesh #DA24
  - Williamsburg blue #DA40
  - Sable brown #DA61
  - Midnite blue #DA85
  - Golden straw #DA168
- Multipurpose sealer from DecoArt
- Paintbrushes:
  - #6 and #8 round bristle
  - #3 soft round
- Zig Memory Systems fine-tip pure brown waterproof writer from EK Success
- 13 flat (½"–¾") metallic gold buttons
- 2 small sprigs imitation greenery
- Tacky craft glue

Project Notes
Refer to photo and pattern throughout.

Let all paints dry between coats and before applying adjacent colors.

See General Instructions on page 188 for detailed directions for painting techniques including base-coating, dry-brushing and rouging.

Instructions
1. Place about 1" water in a small saucepan; add tea bag and bring to a boil. Remove pan from heat and submerge doily in liquid. Soak until doily is slightly darker than desired.

2. Rinse doily in clean water; wring out gently. Air-dry on paper towels for a more aged look, or dry in dryer for more even coloring. Doily will shrink as it dries.

3. Make sure can lid is clean and dry; inside of lid will be right side for painting. Paint lid with sealer; let dry.

4. Base-coat lid and wooden plug with hi-lite flesh. Referring to pattern, base-coat hair with golden straw; rouge cheeks with country red. Dry-brush edges of both lid and plug with sable brown. Add smile, lines around hair and eyes with brown writer.

5. Base-coat outer surfaces of box and lid with Williamsburg blue. Dry-brush edges of box and lid with midnite blue. With brown writer, draw "stitching lines" close to edges on top and sides of lid.

6. Place lid on box. Glue 12 gold

buttons randomly around sides of box bottom; check as they dry to make sure they don't shift. Remove lid; on sides of box, use brown marker to draw eight uneven "stitching lines" radiating from the center of each button.

7. Glue doily to center top of lid. Draw "stitching line" on box lid close to edge of doily with brown writer. Glue face to center of doily; glue wooden plug "nose" to face. Glue greenery over hair at top left of head; glue remaining button over greenery. ✳

Angel Heart Box

Wings of checkered fabric, a barn-red "gown" and dried moss "hair" give this country-style angel lots of down-home charm.

Angel Box

Design by Bonnie Stephens

Materials

- Snowman box from Provo Craft
- 2 wooden 1" primitive stars from Woodworks Inc.
- Fabrics in country-style check:
  2" x 1-yard strip dark green check
  Scraps of barn red check
- Ceramcoat all-purpose sealer from Delta Technical Coatings
- Ceramcoat acrylic paints from Delta Technical Coatings:
  Palomino tan #2108
  Medium flesh #2126
  Barn red #2490
  White #2505
  Black #2506
- Satin-finish interior varnish
- Loew-Cornell paintbrushes:
  #1 Jackie Shaw liner
  ¾" flat wash #7150
  #10 flat #7300
  Spatter brush
  #1 stencil brush
- Stylus
- Dried Spanish moss
- Imitation greenery
- Quick and Easy Tacky glue from Delta Technical Coatings
- 12" (18-gauge) black craft wire
- Sandpaper
- Paper towels
- Black permanent marking pen
- Needle-nose pliers
- Hot-glue gun

Project Notes

Refer to photo throughout, repeating all steps on second side of box.

Let sealer, paints and varnish dry between applications.

Use ¾" flat paintbrush unless instructed otherwise.

Instructions

1. Remove jute twine from box. Apply sealer to all surfaces of box. Sand when dry.

2. Paint all surfaces except head with barn red; paint head medium flesh.

3. Referring to pattern (page 85), outline arms using liner brush and black paint thinned with water. Using #10 flat brush, paint hands with medium flesh; outline hands with thinned black paint and liner.

4. Dot on eyes with stylus dipped in undiluted black paint, redipping before adding second eye.

5. Dip stencil brush in barn red; wipe brush on paper towel to remove most of paint. Color cheeks by rubbing nearly dry brush on face in a circular motion.

6. Paint stars palomino tan; using liner and thinned black paint, add "stitching line" around outer edge.

7. Glue star to neck. Glue Spanish moss hair to head. Tie scraps of barn red checked fabric in simple knot; trim ends and glue to hair. Cut green fabric strip in half; tie each into a bow and glue behind angel for wings.

8. Thin a small amount of white paint with water; using spatter brush, spatter box with mixture. Using same thinned paint, write "Merry Christmas" on box with liner.

9. Coat painted surfaces with one or two coats satin-finish interior varnish.

10. Kink wire as desired; bend into handle and thread ends through holes in sides of box, crimping ends with pliers. ✳

Pattern on page 85

Project Note

Refer to photo throughout.

Angel

1. Peel backing (printed side) from adhesive sheet and apply to back of white fabric. Referring to pattern (page 85), paint angel on front of adhesive-backed fabric using hi-lite flesh for face, baby blue for robe, golden straw for hair, white for wings and emperor's gold for halo.

2. Dip dry stencil or bristle brush in true red paint. Wipe brush on paper towel until almost completely dry, with no brushstrokes showing. Rub nearly dry brush on cheeks in a circular motion.

3. Dot eyes with bullet tip of black writer using side of tip. Using fine tip, add outline and all other details.

4. Using regular scissors, cut out angel along outside edge. Peel off paper backing and stick angel to jar about 1" above bottom of jar.

5. Tie gold floss in a small bow; trim ends even. Glue bow to center front of angel at neck edge.

Jar Topper

1. Using pinking shears through step 2, cut 6" circle from light blue fabric. Spread glue around side of lid. Place clump of fiberfill on jar lid and place fabric circle on top, pressing circle into glue on side of lid (center of fabric should be at center top of lid).

2. Cut 2" x 40" strip of netting. Sew basting stitch lengthwise through center of strip; pull stitches tightly to gather. Wrap gathered netting around side of jar lid; knot thread ends together. Glue net to side of lid; screw lid onto jar.

3. Wrap wire-edge gold ribbon around side of lid. Tie in a bow at center front, concealing gathered edge of netting under ribbon. Trim bow ends even and shape bow. Fill jar with treats. ✳

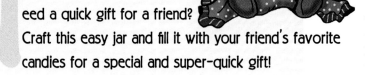

eed a quick gift for a friend? Craft this easy jar and fill it with your friend's favorite candies for a special and super-quick gift!

Angel Jar

Design by Mary Ayres

Materials

- Recycled quart jar with lid (mayonnaise jar works great)
- 4" x 5" piece white cotton fabric
- 4" x 5" PeelnStick double-sided adhesive from Therm O Web
- 7" square textured or solid light blue fabric
- ⅛ yard white bridal netting
- 1 yard (⅜"-wide) metallic gold wire-edge ribbon
- Metallic gold embroidery floss
- Americana acrylic paints from DecoArt:
  Hi-lite flesh #DA24
  Baby blue #DA42
  True red #DA129
  Golden straw #DA168
- White #DSP1 Shimmering Pearls acrylic fabric paint from DecoArt
- Emperor's gold #DA148 Dazzling Metallics acrylic paint from DecoArt
- Paintbrushes:
  #6 round bristle
  ⅛" stencil
  #3 soft round
- Zig Memory System twin-tip pure black writer from EK Success
- Polyester fiberfill
- Pinking shears
- Hand-sewing needle and thread
- Tacky glue
- Paper towels

Pattern on page 85

H

er arms open wide to give you a hug, this angel wears cheerful print robes and Battenburg wings.

Angel Ornament

Design by Mary Ayres

Materials

- Woodsies wooden products from Forster Inc.:
  Jumbo craft stick
  2 mini craft sticks
- 1⅛" x 1¾" wooden split pigeon egg from Lara's Crafts
- Wooden toothpick (optional)
- 2 (4") Battenburg hearts from Wimpole Street Creations
- 3¼" x 6" pinked rectangle print fabric
- ⅝ yard narrow metallic gold braid or trim
- Natural jute twine
- Americana acrylic paints from DecoArt:

White wash #DA2
Flesh tone #DA78
True red #DA129

- Emperor's gold #DA148 Dazzling Metallics acrylic paint from DecoArt
- Paintbrushes:
  2 #6 round bristle brushes
  #3 soft round
- Zig Memory Systems twin-tip pure black writer from EK Success
- Hand-sewing needle and black thread
- Tacky craft glue
- Paper towels
- Craft drill with ³⁄₃₂" bit
- Scrap wood

Project Notes

Refer to photo and pattern (page 84) throughout.

Let all paints dry between coats and before applying adjacent colors.

See General Instructions on page 188 for detailed directions for painting techniques including base-coating and rouging.

Instructions

1. Referring to pattern throughout, lay mini craft sticks (arms) on top of scrap wood and drill holes in ends where indicated. Lightly pencil curved line that separates shoes from legs onto end of jumbo craft stick.

2. Base-coat wooden pieces with two coats of paint as follows: *split-egg head, body/leg area on jumbo craft stick, and mini craft stick*

arms—flesh tone; *"shoes" on jumbo craft stick*—emperor's gold.

3. Lightly pencil facial details onto rounded surface of split egg and leg/shoe details onto jumbo craft stick. Rouge cheeks with true red; add eye dots with bullet tip of black writer. Draw mouth, leg and shoe details with fine tip. Paint a dot of white wash in each eye and cheek using tip of paintbrush handle or toothpick. Glue flat surface of head to top of jumbo craft stick.

4. For bangs, cut several ¾" pieces of jute twine. Separate strands and glue lengthwise across top of head. Trim bangs evenly just above eyes. For hair, cut four 3½" pieces jute twine; lay in a bundle, ends even. Wrap a length of tan thread around center of bundle; knot tightly to

secure. Separate jute strands; glue across top and sides of hair with center of hair at center top of head. Trim ends evenly.

5. For dress, fold fabric in half lengthwise, right sides facing. Sew short sides together using ¼" seam allowance; turn right side out. Sew basting stitch around one long side close to edge, beginning at center back (neck edge). Place dress on craft stick body; pull stitches tightly to gather and knot ends in back. Bring dress gathers around to front under head. Glue top back of dress to jumbo craft stick. Glue mini craft-stick arms to back of dress.

6. From gold cord cut 3¼" piece for halo and 10" piece for hanger. Wrap remaining cord around arms and top of dress, crossing it over angel's chest in an X; glue ends in back. Glue halo around top of head, tilting it slightly to one side and butting ends together.

7. Glue Battenburg hearts to back of angel for wings, overlapping edges; points of hearts should point down and out.

8. Insert ends of hanger cord through angel's hands from front to back; tie knots in ends of cord and top with dots of glue to secure them. ✳

Pattern on page 84

H ung across a mantel or over a doorway, this delightful woodcraft project is decorated with angels, trees, stars and many country add-ons!

Country Christmas Garland

Design by Bonnie Stephens

Materials

♥ Wooden cutouts from Provo Craft:
  3 (4" x 7") angel shapes
  3 (5⅞" x 2") angel wings shapes
  2 (3" x 6") Christmas trees

♥ Wooden shapes from WoodWorks:
  2 (1" x ⅞") primitive stars
  2 (1¼" x 1⅜") primitive stars
  ½" heart

♥ Ceramcoat acrylic sealer from Delta Technical Coatings

♥ Ceramcoat acrylic paints from Delta Technical Coatings:
  Antique white #2001
  Burnt umber #2025
  Palomino tan #2108
  Medium flesh #2126
  Liberty blue #2416
  Hunter green #2471
  Barn red #2490
  Black #2506

♥ Ceramcoat satin interior varnish from Delta Technical Coatings

♥ Loew-Cornell paintbrushes:

  ¾" flat #7150 wash
  #12 flat #7300
  #1 liner
  #1 stencil brush

♥ Stylus

♥ Pencil with new eraser

♥ Sandpaper

♥ 18-gauge black craft wire

♥ Needle-nose pliers

♥ Fabric scraps in various country prints and plaids

♥ Fine-point black permanent marking pen

Project Notes

Refer to photo throughout.

Let sealer, paints, ink and varnish dry between applications.

Use ¾" flat paintbrush unless instructed otherwise.

Painting

1. Apply sealer to all wooden pieces. Sand.

2. Paint pieces as follows: *all angel wings*—antique white; *one angel's gown*—liberty blue; *one angel's gown and all stars*—palomino tan; *one angel's gown and heart*—barn red; *tree trunks*—burnt umber; *trees*—hunter green; *angels' faces, hands and feet*—medium flesh. Sand lightly.

3. Dot eyes of black paint onto each angel using stylus, redipping each time so eyes will be the same size.

4. Dip stencil brush in barn red; wipe on paper towels until brush is almost dry. Scrub face in a circular motion with nearly dry brush to create cheeks.

5. For hair, dip eraser end of pencil into burnt umber; make center dot at top of angel's head, positioning only about half of eraser "stamp" on wood; add remaining dots down sides of head, making them increasingly smaller.

6. Load one side of #12 flat brush with burnt umber and blend on palette. Color should blend from one side of brush to gradually no color on other side of brush. Shade edges of each wing, and shade down center of legs with side-loaded brush.

7. Using antique white and #12 flat brush, paint band near bottom of each dress (add a second coat if necessary to cover gown's base color). Add three clusters of three berries each with stylus dipped in barn red; add small leaves beside berry clusters using liner brush and hunter green.

8. Using stylus, dot ornaments of various colors and sizes onto trees.

9. With marking pen, outline barn red and liberty blue gowns, wings and stars with dashed black lines; add swirls and gathers to palomino tan gown.

Assembly

1. Glue larger stars to tops of trees; glue smaller stars at necklines of barn red and liberty blue gowns; glue heart at neckline of palomino tan dress. Glue wings to back of each angel.

2. Apply one or two coats of satin varnish to all painted wood pieces.

3. Cut wire into 6" pieces; wire angels and trees together with palomino tan angel in center, curling and kinking wire ends to front of garland with needle-nose pliers and adding hanging loops on end pieces.

4. Tear narrow strips from fabrics; tie onto wires. ✻

B

ird lovers and angel collectors alike will adore this sweet angel whose special job is watching over our feathered friends.

Bird-Friendly Angel

Design by Barbara Bennett

Materials

- Sculpey polymer clay: white, beige, tan, brown, red, light blue pearl and yellow
- 2 (1") gold eye pins
- Gold jump ring
- 20-gauge gold craft wire
- Small silk ivy leaves
- Dried Spanish moss
- Acrylic paints: black and white
- Liner brush
- Gareosol clear gloss finish
- Aluminum foil
- Baking sheet
- Palette knife
- Rolling pin
- Rubber gloves
- Toothpick
- Drinking straw
- Pink powdered cosmetic blusher
- Cotton-tip swab
- Oven
- Hot-glue gun
- Pliers

Project Notes

Refer to photo throughout.

Form polymer clay figures directly on foil-lined baking sheet.

Angel is formed and baked on a solid cone of foil. The base of the foil cone must be flat and even for figure to stand straight.

Before shaping polymer clay, knead it between your fingers until pliable. Roll clay an even ¼" thick before cutting flat pieces like gown and wings with palette knife; smooth cut edges with fingers.

Clean hands, rolling pin and work surface thoroughly when changing colors of clay.

Join pieces by pressing them together gently. If not joined securely, pieces will disassemble as they bake.

Sculpting

1. Form smooth, solid cone of aluminum foil 4" tall and 1¾" wide at base.

2. Referring to patterns and detail diagrams (page 86) throughout, cut gown from white polymer clay rolled ¼" thick. Wrap piece around cone, overlapping edges in back. Press seam together gently; trim away excess clay so angel stands straight and balanced.

3. For sleeves, roll two 2" "logs" from white. Slightly taper one end of each and flatten opposite end. Join tapered end to neckline, bending right arm slightly to hold birdhouse. Using the end of drinking straw, imprint circular pattern all over gown and sleeves.

4. From beige, form two ⅜" oval balls for hands; position at ends of sleeves. Insert eye pin in bottom of left hand.

5. From beige, form 1¼" ball for head and ⅛" ball for nose. Press head on top of body over point of cone; press nose onto center of face. For mouth, poke toothpick into clay below nose. Using cotton swab, apply blusher to cheeks.

6. Marbleized wings: Roll thin

snake of clay, ¼" thick x 4" long, from light blue pearl clay; repeat with white and red. Lay snakes side by side; twist and roll together into a long swirl. Roll into a short log and twist until an attractive swirled effect is achieved; do not overmix, as colors will blend together. Roll clay ¼" thick; cut out two wings, reversing one.

Birdhouses, Bird & Halo

1. *Birdhouses:* Cut birdhouse from rolled light blue pearl clay. For roof, roll ½" ball of brown clay into a ⅛" log. Flatten slightly and attach over top of house; trim ends. Roll red clay and brown clay ⅛" thick; cut small heart from red and press onto top of birdhouse; cut circle from brown using end of drinking straw and press onto birdhouse for opening. Poke toothpick into clay to

Continued on page 86

This eye-catching project will remind your family and friends to treat life as a most precious gift!

"Life Is Fragile" Wall Hanging

Design by Barbara Bennett

Materials
- Cernit polymer clay: blue-gray, green, flesh, white, brown, gold and bordeaux
- 7" heart-shaped pine plaque
- Coordinating fabric scrap in print or plaid
- Folk Art antiquing medium
- Acrylic paints: black, white and red
- Liner brush
- Gareosol clear gloss finish
- Jute twine
- Craft drill with ³/₁₆" bit
- Baking sheet lined with aluminum foil
- Garlic press
- Palette knife
- Rolling pin
- Rubber gloves
- Sandpaper
- Soft cloth
- Toothpick
- Pink powdered cosmetic blusher
- Cotton-tip swab
- Oven
- Hot-glue gun

Project Notes
Refer to photo throughout.

Before shaping polymer clay, knead it between your fingers until it is pli-able. Roll clay an even ¼" thick before cutting flat pieces like dresses, wings and stars using palette knife; smooth cut edges with fingers. Form polymer clay figures directly on foil-lined baking sheet.

Clean hands, rolling pin and work surface thoroughly when changing colors of clay.

Join pieces by pressing them together gently. If not joined securely, pieces will disassemble as they bake.

Plaque
1. Lightly sand all surfaces of plaque; wipe off dust. While wearing rubber gloves, rub antiquing medium over all surfaces of plaque with soft cloth; let dry.

2. For hanger, drill two holes in center top of plaque; thread jute twine through holes from back to front. Tie a knot in each end; trim ends.

Bordeaux Angel
1. Referring to patterns and assembly diagrams (page 92) throughout, cut dress from bordeaux polymer clay rolled ¼" thick. For sleeves, roll two 1"-long, ¼"-diameter "logs" from bordeaux. Carefully place one sleeve behind neckline of dress, extending arm out to left. Place remaining sleeve across front of dress, stretching arms gently to meet.

2. Using flesh polymer clay through-out, form two ¼" balls; attach one to end of each sleeve for hand. Form

two 1"-long, ⅛"-diameter logs for legs; position at an angle beneath lower portion of dress. Form ½" ball for head; flatten slightly and attach at dress neckline. Roll very tiny ball for nose and join to center of face. Using cotton swab, apply blusher to cheeks.

3. From rolled white polymer clay, cut one wing; press to back of dress opposite sleeves. Using tip of tooth-pick, dot a line of impressions around outer edge of wing.

4. For hair, squeeze pliable brown polymer clay through garlic press; cut off ¼" lengths using toothpick. Arrange strands around head, work-ing from back to front and along shoulders and wing.

5. For halo, roll very thin string of gold polymer clay; form in circle at top of head.

Green Angel
In general, follow steps 1–5 for Bordeaux Angel, substituting green polymer clay for bordeaux. As shown in pattern on page 92, reverse dress, wing and arms to right, and position arms closer together.

Blue-Gray Angel
In general, follow steps 1–5 for Bordeaux Angel, substituting blue-gray polymer clay for bordeaux. Make other changes as follows:

1. Position body to face center front. Slightly taper one end of each sleeve

Continued on page 89

E ncircle your Christmas tree with this cheerful no-sew tree skirt adorned with fused angels and stars! And craft yourself a vest or two for sharing holiday cheer!

Jute Angel Tree Skirt & Denim Vests

Designs by Angie Wilhite

Materials
Tree Skirt

♥ 45" round jute tree skirt
♥ Fabrics:
  ⅓ yard cream print
  ⅓ yard each of 2 hunter green prints (A)
  ¼ yard contrasting hunter green print (B)
  ⅓ yard each of 3 burgundy prints
  ⅛ yard flesh tone
  ⅛ yard blue check or print
  ⅛ yard gold print
♥ Marbled tan 4-hole buttons:
  25 (⅜")
  10 (¼")
♥ 1½ yards HeatnBond Ultra Hold iron-on adhesive from Therm O Web
♥ Therm O Web pressing paper
♥ Fabri-Tac permanent fabric adhesive from Beacon Adhesives
♥ 2⅔ yards jute twine

Angel Vests
♥ Adult- and child-size denim vests
♥ Fabrics:
  Light gold print

Dark gold print
2 burgundy prints
Green print
Flesh tone
♥ Marbled tan 4-hole buttons:
  8 (⅜") for adult's vest
  3 (⅜") for child's vest
♥ Matching Coats' Dual-Duty Plus rayon embroidery threads
♥ Matching all-purpose sewing threads
♥ 2 yards Pellon Wonder Under transfer fusing web
♥ 1 yard Pellon Sof-Shape fusible interfacing
♥ 2½ yards Pellon Stitch-n-Tear fabric stabilizer
♥ Hand-sewing needle
♥ Sewing machine

All Projects
♥ Fine-point black permanent fabric-marking pen
♥ Fabri-Tac permanent adhesive from Beacon Adhesives
♥ Cotton-tip swab
♥ Pink powdered cosmetic blusher
♥ Iron

Project Notes
Refer to photo throughout.

Patterns given (page 87) are correct size for child's vest and for motifs on front of adult's vest. Using

photocopier with enlarging capabilities, enlarge all patterns for angels, stars and moon 155 percent before cutting pieces for tree skirt and for

Continued on page 87

Craft this darling angel to watch over your sweetest little treasures day and night!

Guardian Angel
Design by Barbara Matthiessen

Materials
- 14" x 10" piece of 1"-thick pine
- 4" x 10" piece of ¾"-thick pine
- Wooden products from Forster Inc.:

  4 Woodsies star cutouts, ⅞"–1¾"

  5 mini clothespins

  2 (¾") circles
- Band saw, scroll saw, saber saw or coping saw
- Craft drill with ⅛" bit
- Medium-grit sandpaper
- Ceramcoat acrylic paints from Delta Technical Coatings:

  Blue jay #2059

  Fleshtone base #2082

  Wild rose #2485

  White #2505

  Black #2506
- Opaque blue #2508
- Paintbrushes: flat shaders and medium stencil brush
- Paper towels
- Pencil with new eraser
- Disposable 4-prong fork
- Oak antiquing medium
- Fine-point black permanent marking pen
- .05 black Pigma marker from Micron
- Krylon Crystal Clear matte acrylic sealer
- Scraps of red "homespun-style" check or print fabric
- Kids Choice Glue from Beacon Adhesives
- 1 yard ⅝"-wide ivory eyelet trim
- Jute twine
- Assorted tiny buttons
- Sawtooth hanger

Project Notes
Refer to photo and pattern (pages 90 and 91) throughout.

Paint front and edges of wooden pieces. Let paints, antiquing medium and sealer dry between coats and before applying adjacent colors.

Painting & Staining
1. Referring to patterns throughout cut angel and banner from 1" pine and wings from ¾" pine. Drill holes where indicated. Sand all edges until smooth.

2. Paint dress and outer border on banner opaque blue. Paint wings and inner portion of banner white. Paint head, hands and wooden rounds fleshtone base.

3. Load a small amount of wild rose on stencil blush; blot off most of paint onto paper towels. Blush cheeks by dabbing and swirling nearly dry brush on wood. Dot on eyes with wooden tip of paintbrush handle dipped in black paint.

4. Dip eraser end of pencil in blue jay; dot randomly over dress. Dip prongs of plastic fork into white paint; apply random rows of dots to dress.

5. Sand off painted edges to give wood a "distressed" look. Sand across painted banner and down painted dress.

6. Using fine-point marker, add lettering and outline details on banner, outline wings and details on dress.

Using .05 marker, add details to face and hands and a border of squiggly lines and dots around stars and painted wooden rounds.

7. Following manufacturer's instructions, apply two coats sealer to all wooden pieces.

8. Brush antiquing medium over banner, wings and dress, wiping off excess before it sets.

Finishing & Assembly
1. Wrap eyelet around angel at bottom, arms and neck and glue to secure. Glue wooden rounds slightly overlapping at center bottom of eyelet trim for feet.

2. Tear 12" x ½" fabric; tie in a bow and glue at angel's neck. Tie small bow from jute twine and glue over fabric bow; glue button over center of jute bow.

3. Cut 18" piece of jute twine; thread through holes in hands and knot so twine hangs in front of angel to form "clothesline" from which photos can be hung. Tie fabric scraps and jute bow to clothesline. Glue clothespins and two smaller stars to garland.

4. Glue angel to wings so holes in wings are ½" above angel's hands.

5. Tear 1½" x 18" strip fabric; tie in a bow. Glue bow to upper corner of banner; glue buttons to center of bow, and glue two wooden stars to banner.

6. Attach sawtooth hanger to center back of banner.

7. Cut two 8" pieces of jute twine. Thread ends from back to front through holes in angel and banner to join the two pieces; double-knot ends. Check to make sure angel hangs evenly. Tie fabric scraps and jute knots. Hang photos from clothespins on line. ✳

Patterns on page 90

Add holiday cheer to your office or casual attire with this simple-to-craft angel pin!

Tiny Angel Pin

Design by Ann Butler

Materials
- ¾" wooden round plug
- Acrylic paints: flesh tone, rose pink and white
- Small paintbrush
- Wooden toothpick
- Fine-point black permanent marking pen
- 2" x 1½" piece fabric in desired print
- 2" x 1½" piece Warm and Natural batting from The Warm Co.
- 1" pin back
- Coordinating embroidery floss or quilting thread
- Hand-sewing needle
- Small amount of Li'l Loopies doll hair
- 3" piece gold 24-gauge craft wire
- Hot-glue gun

Project Notes
Refer to photo throughout.

Let all paints dry between coats.

Instructions
1. Paint wooden plug with flesh-tone paint. Referring to pattern throughout, add round cheeks of rose pink paint; using tip of tooth-pick, dot tiny white highlight onto each cheek. Draw eyes with fine-line marking pen.

2. Cut one heart from fabric and one from batting. Lay fabric atop batting; pin together.

Tiny Angel Pin

3. Blanket-stitch around hearts with needle and thread. Sew pin back to batting side of assembled hearts.

4. Wind doll hair around three or four fingers 12–15 times; slide loops off hand and tie around middle with another piece of hair or matching thread. Clip loops and glue hair to angel's head. Trim ends.

5. For halo, bend wire into a ½"-diameter circle; twist ends together; glue halo stem to back of head and bend halo to front.

6. Glue head to fabric "wings." ✳

With one delightful pattern, you can create a collection of ornaments, a plant poke, or many other accents to dress up your holiday home!

Paper-Craft Angel Accents

Design by Helen L. Rafson

Materials

Each Angel
- 3 (7") squares cut from heavy brown paper bag
- Tacky craft glue
- Fusible web
- Fabric scraps: pink solid, white print, and colorful print/pattern of your choice
- Black acrylic paint
- Small paintbrush
- Fine-point black permanent marking pen
- Pink powdered cosmetic blusher
- Cotton-tip swab
- 6 assorted (⅜"–½") buttons in color(s) desired for hair
- 7⅞" piece (⅛"-wide) coordinating satin ribbon

Ornament
- 9" piece (⅛"-wide) gold ribbon

Plant Poke
- 15" (¼"-diameter) wooden dowel
- 3 strands natural raffia

Project Notes

Refer to photo throughout.

Cut out pieces with regular scissors unless instructed otherwise.

Let all glue, ink and paints dry before proceeding with next step.

Instructions

1. Glue paper squares together in layers, matching edges. Referring to patterns (page 93), cut angel outline from layered brown paper.

2. Following manufacturer's instructions, fuse web to wrong side of fabrics; referring to patterns, cut robe from colorful print, two hands, two feet and one face from pink and, using pinking shears, cut wings from fused white print fabric.

3. Dip end of paintbrush handle into black paint; dot eyes onto fabric face.

4. Using fine-point marking pen, add eyelashes and mouth. Apply blusher to cheeks with cotton swab.

5. Check position of pattern pieces on brown paper outline. Fuse pieces in place in order: wings, hands, feet, gown and face.

6. Glue buttons around face for hair.

7. Tie ribbon in bow; cut ends at an angle. Glue bow at neckline.

Ornament Finishing

Fold gold ribbon in half; glue ends to back of angel for hanging loop.

Plant Poke Finishing

Glue about 1½" of blunt end of skewer to back of angel. Tie 3 strands raffia in a bow around dowel about 1" below angel. ✻

Patterns on page 93

T

his sweet country angel with her string of colored lights will add the crowning touch to your Christmas tree!

Christmas Angel Tree Topper

Design by Veleta Stafney

Materials
- Clean, empty, 32-ounce plastic soda bottle with cap
- 2 sheets white felt
- 1¾" wooden ball knob
- ¼" wooden furniture button
- Ceramcoat acrylic paints from Delta Technical Coatings:
  Adobe red #2046
  Medium flesh #2126
  White #2505
  Black #2506
- Ceramcoat satin-finish varnish from Delta Technical Coatings
- Paintbrush
- Stylus
- Toothpick
- Cotton-tip swab
- Fine-point black permanent marking pen
- 1½-yard x 6" strip white tulle
- ½ yard red, green and gold-striped fabric
- 1¾ yards (½"-wide) white ruffled lace
- Polyester fiberfill
- Coordinating sewing threads and hand-sewing needle
- 4" white Battenburg lace heart from Wimpole Street Creations
- Strawberry & Sandy two-tone Mini-Curl doll hair from One & Only Creations
- 18" metallic gold wired star garland
- 1" metallic gold satin heart
- 1 set (2¼" x 5½") metallic gold puffy fabric wings
- ½ yard (⅛"-wide) red satin ribbon
- String of miniature Christmas tree lights
- Fabri-Tac fabric glue from Beacon Adhesives
- Serrated knife
- Sewing machine (optional)
- Iron

Project Notes
Refer to photo throughout.

Let paints, ink and varnish dry between applications.

Test marking pen with varnish on a scrap of wood to make sure varnish will not make marker run. Thinned black acrylic paint applied with a liner brush may be substituted for marker.

Use ¾" seam allowance throughout, and backstitch at beginnings and ends of seams. Clip off excess thread ends from sewing and gathering stitches.

Bottle
1. Using serrated knife, cut bottom ½" from soda bottle. Apply a dab of glue inside bottle cap and replace on bottle.

2. Referring to pattern (page 94), cut two bottle covers from white felt. With right sides facing, sew covers together along sides leaving top and bottom open; turn right side out. Sew basting stitch along neck edge. Slip cover over bottle and pull basting stitch to gather fabric snugly around bottleneck; knot thread.

3. Apply a line of glue inside bottom edge of bottle; fold felt up inside bottle and press into glue.

Head
1. Referring to Fig. 1 (page 94), glue furniture button (nose) to wooden ball knob (head); paint nose and head with medium flesh. Dot on eyes using stylus dipped in black paint. Dip cotton-tip swab in adobe red; lightly brush cheeks and nose.

2. With fine-point marking pen, draw eyelashes and mouth; add freckles to cheeks and nose. With tip of toothpick, add tiny white highlight dot to each cheek and eye.

3. Coat head with one or two coats of varnish; glue to top of bottle cap.

Slip & Gown
1. *Slip:* Hand-sew basting stitch along one long edge of tulle. Place around body 5" from bottom of bottle (basting stitch should be along top edge); pull thread to gather tulle around bottle. Distribute gathers evenly around bottle; knot thread.

2. *Gown:* Cut one piece of fabric 9½" x 45". Turn under ¼" hem along one long edge; iron. Sew lace to wrong side of hem. Right sides facing, sew short ends together. Turn under top long edge ¼" and sew basting stitch along fold; turn right side out. Place dress over bottle, positioning top edge of fabric (with gathering stitch) right under bottle cap. Pull gathers tight; knot thread.

3. *Arms:* Cut one piece fabric 6" x 11". Turn under ¼" along each 6" edge. Sew lace to wrong side of each hem. Fold arm strip in half lengthwise right sides facing and seam long edges to make tube. Turn right side out. Referring to Fig. 2 (page 94), sew gathering stitch crosswise across center of arm tube. Pull gathers tight; knot thread.

4. Lightly stuff each arm through open cuff end. Sew basting stitch

Continued on page 94

Baking Christmas cookies will be all the more fun for you and your family when you don this festive apron!

Gingerbread Angel Apron

Design by Kathy Wegner

Materials
- Adult-size canvas apron
- Fabric-marking pencil or air-soluble fabric marker
- Small sponges
- Scribbles 3-D paints from Duncan Enterprises:
  Shiny white #SC110
  Shiny gingersnap #SC137
  Shiny tea #SC166
  Crystal gel very berry red #SC513
- Small flat paintbrush
- Fine-point black permanent fabric-marking pen
- Seed beads in assorted colors
- Cardboard covered with plastic wrap or T-shirt painting board
- Paper towels
- Toothpick

Project Notes
Refer to photo throughout.

To make each tiny heart, squeeze two dots of paint side by side. Using toothpick, pull paint down from each dot to make point of heart.

Instructions
1. Launder apron without using fabric softener; dry and press as needed.

2. Referring to pattern (page 95), reproduce pattern and lettering on

apron using fabric-marking pencil or air-soluble pen. Place apron on cardboard.

3. Dampen sponge with water; squeeze dry. Dip sponge in shiny tea paint; blot off excess onto paper towel. Dab sponge on heart on apron; repeat as needed to fill in heart.

4. Using clean sponge, repeat sponging technique to fill gingerbread man with shiny gingersnap paint.

5. Dip small brush in shiny gingerbread paint; blot off excess paint. Dab brush around wing edges; let dry.

6. Squeeze very berry red paint onto heart leaving a narrow, uneven

tea-stained edge showing; let dry. Using technique described in Project Notes, make tiny very berry red hearts around gingerbread angel and to dot the i in "is."

7. Squeeze shiny white paint on inner surfaces of wings; drop seed beads into wet paint for "sprinkles"; let dry.

8. Outline gingerbread angel, heart, face and lettering with permanent fabric marker. Let paints and ink dry for at least 24 hours before wearing, and at least 72 hours before laundering. ✳

Pattern on page 95

Hang this pair of enchanting angels on your tree for a sweet country touch.

Wooden Spoon Angel Ornaments

Design by Chris Malone

Materials
Each Angel Ornament
- Woodsies wooden products from Forster Inc.:
  Craft spoon
  4 mini craft sticks
  2 large (2"-long) teardrops
  Large (1⁵⁄₁₆") circle
  Large (1⅝") star
- ⅛ yard of print fabric
- Hand-sewing needle and matching thread
- Sewing machine (optional)
- 10" piece (⅜"-wide) white wire-edged ribbon
- 12" piece (⅛"-wide) white satin ribbon
- Brown Mini Curl doll hair from One & Only Creations
- Acrylic paints: white, desired flesh tone, dark flesh tone for shading, gold and black
- Paintbrushes: flat and small stencil brush
- Paper towels
- Satin-finish varnish
- Hot-glue gun

Project Notes
Refer to photo throughout.

Let paints and varnish dry between coats.

Painting
1. Base-coat wooden pieces with two coats of paint as follows: *teardrops (wings)*—white; *star and circle (star and halo)*—gold; *spoon and mini craft sticks (body/head, arms and legs)*—flesh tone.

2. For eyes, dip tip of paintbrush handle into black; touch to face (bowl of spoon). Redip for second eye so eyes are the same size. For cheeks, dip stencil brush into shading flesh tone; dab most of paint off onto paper towels, then tap brush on face.

3. Coat all painted pieces with satin-finish varnish.

Assembly
1. Glue tops of two legs (two mini craft sticks) side by side to handle of spoon.

2. Cut 8½" x 4" rectangle from fabric; fold in half, right sides facing, and sew short ends together by hand or machine, leaving ¼" seam allowance. Press ¼" hem at each end. Starting at seam (center back), hand-sew gathering stitch around each end ⅛" from fold of hem. Slip tube dress over body; position neckline 1¼" below top of head and bottom hem 1" above ends of legs. Pull gathers so dress fits snugly at both ends and pouts out slightly in middle. Hold dress in place with a few dots of glue.

3. Referring to pattern, cut four sleeves from remaining fabric. Pin sleeves together in pairs, right sides facing; sew each pair together by hand or machine, using ¼" seam allowance and leaving bottoms open.

Press ¼" hem at bottom; hand-sew gathering stitch around opening ⅛" from fold; repeat for remaining sleeve. Turn sleeves right side out.

4. Apply glue to tip of one arm; insert into sleeve so top of arm is attached in top of sleeve. Pull gathering stitch so sleeve fits snugly around hand. Repeat with remaining sleeve and arm. Glue top of each completed sleeve to front neckline at an angle.

5. Frizz curly hair by rubbing it gently between fingertips. Apply glue to top of head; gently press curls in place, adding hair as desired.

6. Apply glue to tips of wings; glue at an angle to back of angel's dress. Glue halo to back of head; glue star to back of one hand.

7. Tie wire-edge ribbon in bow; arrange ends and trim as desired; glue at angel's neck.

8. Make hanging loop by knotting ends of satin ribbon together. Glue knot to back of angel above wings. If angel doesn't hang straight, apply additional glue to ribbon at back of halo. ✳

S elect a variety of pretty country-style papers and create your own collection of unique cards and gift bags to give to family and friends.

Paper Angel Bag & Cards

Design by Kathy Wegner

Materials
- 6½" x 5" blank white greeting card with envelope
- 8½" x 5½" kraft paper gift bag with handles
- 9¾" x 7¾" white paper gift bag with handles
- Mounting Memories Keepsake Glue from Beacon Adhesives
- Paper in desired solid color for hands and faces
- Printed scrapbook papers in assorted colors and designs
- Paper edgers in desired pattern(s)
- Permanent marking pens:
  Brown
  Fine-point black
- Red colored pencil

Project Notes
Refer to photo throughout.

If using striped or plaid paper for dress and sleeves, cut sleeves with lines in opposite direction. Or use contrasting paper for sleeves, as shown on angels on white gift bag.

Instructions
1. Referring to patterns (page 96), cut face and hands for each angel from paper of desired solid color,

cutting bottom edge of each dress with paper edgers. Cut wings, sleeves and dress for each angel from desired printed papers, reversing dresses as desired.

2. Plan placement of pieces on gift card or bag. Glue wings to bag or card first. Glue hands to sleeves; slip sleeves over dress top and glue in place. Glue dress to wings and glue head above dress.

3. Color cheeks lightly with red pencil. Using black marker, add eyes, dashes between lines, and dashed outline on wings. Using brown marker, draw hair as shown. ✳

Patterns on page 96

Filled with pinecones and holly or a special present, this country basket makes a lovely decoration to make and share!

Angel With Heart Basket

Design by Chris Malone

Materials
- Coordinating fabrics:
  10" square red-and-tan mini check
  4" square tea-dyed or tan muslin
  6" x 8" piece red-and-tan print
- Matching sewing threads
- Hand-sewing needle
- Sewing machine (optional)
- Polyester fiberfill
- Rose powdered cosmetic blusher
- Cotton-tip swab
- 6" x 4" piece fleece
- 6-strand embroidery floss: brown and red
- Brown Raf-A-Doodle Petite Locks curled raffia doll hair from One & Only Creations
- 1" piece tan lace trim
- 1½" wooden primitive heart
- Red acrylic paint
- Paintbrush
- 5 strands natural raffia
- Basket with handle (see Project Notes)
- Hot-glue gun

Project Notes
Refer to photo throughout.

Basket used for sample is a round basket 9½" in diameter and 13" tall.

Angel
1. Referring to patterns (page 97), cut two bodies, reversing one, from checked fabric.

2. Fold remaining checked fabric, muslin and print fabric in half, right sides facing; trace two arms onto doubled checked fabric, one head and two legs onto doubled muslin, and one set of wings onto doubled print fabric. Secure fabric layers with pins.

3. By hand or machine, sew around head and legs on traced lines, leaving openings where indicated. Cut out ⅛" from seam; clip curves and turn right side out. Stuff firmly with polyester fiberfill; baste openings closed.

4. Pin body halves together, right sides facing. Insert legs between layers where indicated (most of legs should be between body layers). Using ¼" seam allowance, sew around body, leaving opening at neck and catching tops of legs in seam. Clip curves; turn right side out. Stuff body with polyester fiberfill.

5. Using 2 strands brown embroidery floss, add French knot eyes to angel's face; using 1 strand, straight stitch eyebrows and nose. Apply blusher to cheeks with cotton-tip swab.

6. Turn neck hem under ¼"; finger press. Slip head into neck opening

and slipstitch all around to hold head in place.

7. Sew arms on traced lines, leaving openings where indicated. Clip curves; turn right side out. Stuff firmly; whipstitch openings closed. Hot-glue arms to shoulders.

8. Lay traced wings on top of fleece; sew around on traced outline through all layers. Cut out ⅛" from seam; clip curves and trim corners. Make slash down center through one fabric layer; turn wings right side out through slash. Whipstitch opening closed.

9. Using 2 strands red floss, sew running stitch around wings ⅜" from edge. Sew line of gathering stitches down center of wings through all layers; pull floss to gather slightly. Glue wings to back of angel with slash facing angel.

10. Cut several 3" pieces of raffia hair. Gently pull apart to fluff curls. Arrange and glue ringlets to top, sides and back of head. Glue lace trim to neckline, concealing seam.

Assembly
1. Paint wooden heart red. Tie natural raffia strands in a bow; trim ends to 3" and glue bow to angel over ends of arms; glue heart to center of bow.

2. Glue angel to basket handle as shown. ✳

Patterns on page 97

E mbellish a simple
T-shirt with fused-on
fabric designs for
a holiday wearable with
angelic charm.

Noel Angel T-Shirt

Design by Barbara A. Woolley

Materials

- Natural-color T-shirt
- Fabric scraps:

  5" x 3" piece Christmasy plaid or print (angel's collar)

  7" x 3" piece dark green with gold accents (letters)

  Small piece of fleshtone (face)

  6" square metallic gold fabric (wings)

  ⅛-yard gold star-print fabric (stars)
- 1 yard Steam-A-Seam 2 adhesive-backed fusible web from The Warm Company
- Small amount of red-brown washable doll hair
- Silver glitter fabric paint writer
- Fine-point black permanent fabric-marking pen
- White fabric paint
- Paintbrush
- Fabric glue
- Small ribbon bow
- Large-eye needle
- Iron

Instructions

1. Launder and dry T-shirt without using fabric softener; press as needed.

2. Referring to patterns (page 98), transfer one collar, one of each of the "NOEL" letters, one face, two wings, reversing one, three star A's, two star B's, four star C's and four star D's to wrong side of fusible transfer web. Following manufacturer's instructions, fuse pattern pieces to backs of fabric: collar onto Christmas print, letters onto dark green, face onto fleshtone; wings onto metallic gold and stars onto gold star print.

3. Cut out pieces. Referring to photo throughout, arrange appliqués on shirt front and fuse in place, placing one star A and one star B to left of angel and one star A, one star C and two star D's to right of angel.

4. Arrange one star A, one star B, one star C and two star D's around neckline on back of shirt; fuse in place.

5. Fuse one star C to side of each sleeve about ½" from edge.

6. Add facial details with black fine-point marking pen. Add tiny dot of white paint to each eye for highlight.

7. Glue bow at angel's neckline.

8. With large-eye needle, sew 5" strands of hair around head; pull hair to sides as shown and gather with additional lengths of doll hair, threading ends of ties through to wrong side of shirt. Secure hair as needed with fabric glue so it will stay in place when shirt is laundered.

9. Add halo with silver glitter paint writer. ✳

Patterns on page 98

C reate an antique-looking keepsake ornament from tea-dyed Battenburg lace and a stencil!

Battenburg Lace Ornament

Design by Rose Pirrone

Materials

- ♥ 2 butter yellow #127DT-4SQ 4" Battenburg lace squares from Wimpole Street Creations
- ♥ American Traditional Tiny Trims angel stencil (moon) #BLT2
- ♥ Cottage blue #90-153-0059 Stencil Magic Stencil Paint Creme from Delta Technical Coatings Inc.
- ♥ ¼" stencil brush
- ♥ Dry potpourri
- ♥ Aleene's No-Sew Fabric Glue
- ♥ 4 small blue blossom appliqués #193 262 0 from Wrights
- ♥ 9" piece (⅜"-wide) light blue satin ribbon
- ♥ Low-tack masking tape
- ♥ Paper towels

Project Notes

Refer to photo throughout.

Allow paints to dry completely as needed to keep from smearing stenciled designs.

Instructions

1. Mask off stars on stencil sheet. Tape stencil to one of the Battenburg lace squares, centering angel in square. Using cottage blue stencil crème and stencil brush, stencil angel onto lace square using a circular motion.

2. Remove stencil. Stencil a small star on each side of square. Allow paint to dry completely.

3. Carefully trim lace edging from second Battenburg square. Holding square pieces back to back, spread glue along edges of three sides; press together.

4. When glue is dry, fill center of pocket with potpourri. Glue opening closed.

5. Glue blossom appliqué in each corner of stenciled panel.

6. For hanger, fold ribbon in loop; glue ends together and glue ends to back of sachet. Allow glue to dry thoroughly before hanging. ✳

B

righten your home with this charming cherub's glittering personality! Pearlescent beads hang from the wings of this heaven-sent delight.

Beaded Angel

Design by Mary Ayres

Materials

- 3" slate circle
- 1¼" wooden furniture button
- White craft foam
- Pony beads:
  20 clear pearl
  10 metallic gold
  2 white pearl
  4 yellow pearl
  4 blue pearl
- 1½ yards white fabric craft cord
- Metallic gold embroidery floss
- Bubble red doll hair from Twice as Nice Designs
- Zig Memory System opaque writers from EK Success: pure black and white
- American acrylic paints from DecoArt:
  Salem blue #DA43
  Flesh tone #DA78
  True red #DA129
  Yellow light #DA144
- Paintbrushes:
  #3 round bristle #6
  Soft round #3
- Fiskars paper edgers: wave and mini pinking
- Tacky craft glue
- ⅛" round paper punch
- Craft drill with ³⁄₃₂" bit
- Scrap wood

Project Notes

Refer to photo throughout.

Let all paints and inks dry between coats and before applying adjacent colors.

See General Instructions on page 188 for detailed directions for painting techniques including rouging.

Instructions

1. Paint all surfaces of wooden button head with flesh tone. Referring to facial diagram (page 96), lightly sketch eyes and smile on rounded surface of buttons. Rouge cheeks with true red. Draw eyes and mouth with black writer.

2. Glue hair to top and sides of head. Tie several strands of metallic gold floss into a small bow; glue to right side of hair.

3. Lay slate flat on scrap of wood; drill two holes through wooden frame ¾" apart for tying on beaded "legs." Paint wooden slate frame Salem blue.

4. Using tip of paintbrush handle, dot evenly spaced yellow light dots onto painted frame. Using black writer, draw a "stitched line" around inside edge of frame close to edge.

5. Referring to lettering diagram (page 96), write "Peace" on slate with opaque white writer, making sure holes for legs are positioned at center bottom.

6. Referring to pattern (page 96), cut wings from white craft foam, using mini pinking edgers to cut top and side edges, and wave edgers to cut bottom edge. Punch holes where indicated using paper punch. Glue wings to back of slate body. Glue head to center top front of body. Let glue dry.

7. Cut eight 4" pieces white cord; knot one end of each piece. Onto each piece thread a clear bead, a gold bead and another clear bead. Insert ends of cords through holes in bottoms of wings from front to back; knot cord ends on back.

8. Cut two 5" pieces white cord for legs; knot one end of each piece. Onto each piece thread a gold bead, a clear bead, a yellow bead, a blue bead, a white bead, a yellow bead and a clear bead. Insert ends of cords through holes in frame from front to back; knot cord ends on back.

9. Cut 9" piece of white cord for hanger; insert ends through holes in tops of wings from front to back; knot ends of cord. ✳

Patterns on page 96

Dress up the front door of your home with this creative angel door decoration!

Christmas Blessings Angel

Design by Bonnie Stephens

Materials
- Wooden Victorian angel from Walnut Hollow
- 4 (4½") ¼"-diameter wooden dowels
- 5 (¾") wooden buttons from Woodworks Inc.
- 2 wooden primitive stars from Woodworks Inc.
- Ceramcoat all-purpose sealer from Delta Technical Coatings
- Ceramcoat acrylic paints from Delta Technical Coatings:
  Antique white #2001
  Light chocolate #2022
  Palomino tan #2108
  Medium flesh #2126
  Liberty blue #2416
  Barn red #2490
  Black #2506
- Ceramcoat brown antiquing gel from Delta Technical Coatings
- Loew-Cornell paintbrushes: ¾" flat wash #7150
- Spatter brush
- #1 stencil brush
- Stylus
- 2" x 6" piece ecru crochet lace
- 5" x 6" piece muslin
- 3½" piece (½"-wide) ecru crochet edging
- Hand-sewing needle and thread
- Dried Spanish moss
- 9" cinnamon stick
- Imitation greenery
- Small scrap of print fabric
- Fine jute twine
- Quick and Tacky glue from Delta Technical Coatings
- 36" (18-gauge) black craft wire
- Sandpaper
- Black permanent marking pen
- Needle-nose pliers
- Craft drill with small bit
- Paper towels

Project Notes
Refer to photo throughout.

Let sealer and paints dry between applications.

Use ¾" flat paintbrush unless instructed otherwise.

Painting
1. Apply sealer to all wood pieces. Sand lightly.

2. Paint two dowels and all areas of wooden angel except head with antique white; paint head and remaining dowels with medium flesh. Paint about ¾" on one end of the antique white dowels with medium flesh for hands. Sand painted pieces to achieve a primitive look, making sure some wood shows through paint.

3. Dip stylus in black paint and dot on eyes, redipping before making second eye.

4. Dip stencil brush in barn red; blot off most of paint onto paper towel until brush is nearly dry. Add blush to cheeks by scrubbing in a circular motion with nearly dry brush.

5. Apply antiquing gel to all painted surfaces; wipe off with paper towel.

6. Using permanent marking pen, draw dashed "stitching line" around edges of wings and angel.

7. Using thinned black paint and spatter brush, spatter angel and wings very lightly.

Assembly
1. Drill two small holes through angel from front to back, positioning holes just below neckline and about ³⁄₁₆" from neck edge. Drill two more holes at center bottom of angel ½" apart and ¼" above edge. Drill small hole crosswise through top of each dowel; also glue small hole crosswise through medium flesh "hand" on each arm dowel.

2. With wire, attach arm dowels through holes at shoulders and neck; attach leg dowels through holes in dowels and at bottom of angel. Curl wire ends with needle-nose pliers to hold dowels in place.

3. With needle and thread, stitch 2"-wide lace to one end of muslin for apron; run gathering stitch across opposite end; pull thread to gather and knot.

4. "Tea-dye" muslin-and-lace apron in a mixture of 1 cup water and a small amount of light chocolate paint; let dry and glue gathered end of apron to angel as shown.

5. Using liner brush, write "Christmas Blessings" across wings.

6. Drill holes for hanger in wings; add hanging loop of wire, curling wire ends with needle-nose pliers.

7. Glue dried Spanish moss to angel's head for hair. Tie knot in center of ½"-wide crochet edging and glue to hair. Tie small bow of jute twine and glue at angel's neck.

Feather Tree & Finishing
1. Cut 1", 2", 4" and 6" strands of imitation greenery. Glue center of each piece to cinnamon stick, positioning shortest piece 1" from top

end and positioning remaining strands about 1¼" apart.

2. *Paint buttons:* one liberty blue, two barn red and two palomino tan; sand edges. Paint wooden stars palomino tan. Glue buttons to "boughs"; glue one star to top of tree and other star over gathers at top of apron. Tie fabric scrap in a knot; glue to tree trunk. Tie small bow of jute twine; glue to tree.

3. Wire tree to angel's hands, threading wire through holes in hands and wrapping it around tree trunk. ✳

S

"nowflakes on your nose are an angel's happy kisses"

reads this decorative tin-punched pie tin.

Angel Kisses Pie Tin

Design by Sandra Graham Smith

Materials

- 9" aluminum pie tin
- Tracing paper
- Masking tape
- Hammer
- Several finishing nails
- Larger carpentry nail
- Pressed-wood board for work surface
- Enamel paints: white, black, yellow, blue, red
- Tulip's gold glitter fabric paint from Duncan Enterprises
- Small paintbrush
- Fine-point permanent marking pens: red, black and white
- 10" piece (⅛"-wide) blue satin ribbon

Project Notes

Refer to photo throughout.

Punching & Painting

1. Trace pattern (page 99) onto tracing paper; cut to fit inside pie pan. Secure pattern with masking tape so it does not shift as you work.

2. Place pan on work surface. Using hammer and finishing nail, punch design, moving from dot to dot and changing nails as tip dulls. Punch two holes with larger nail at top for hanger. Remove pattern and tape.

3. Apply acrylic paints inside

punched lines with paintbrush, using thick strokes and referring to pattern and photo. Mix white and blue paints to make light blue, and white and red paints to make pink. Let paint dry completely.

4. Apply gold glitter paint to halos. Paint yellow buttons on boy's suspenders. Add a little red to pink paint to make a darker pink; use this mixture to paint round cheeks on boy and girl.

Finishing

1. Using white marking pen, add stitch lines around patch on boy's overalls. Draw "plaid" lines on blue star and add dots and lines to red heart.

2. Using red marking pen, draw smiles on both angels.

3. Using black marking pen, draw round eyes on both angels and dot tiny buttonholes on boy's buttons. Add stitching line around neckline and hem of girl's apron. Write "Snowflakes on your nose are an angel's happy kisses" on painted white band, adding dots on ends of letters.

4. For hanger, thread ribbon through larger holes in top of pie pan; tie ends together in a bow. ✳

Pattern on page 99

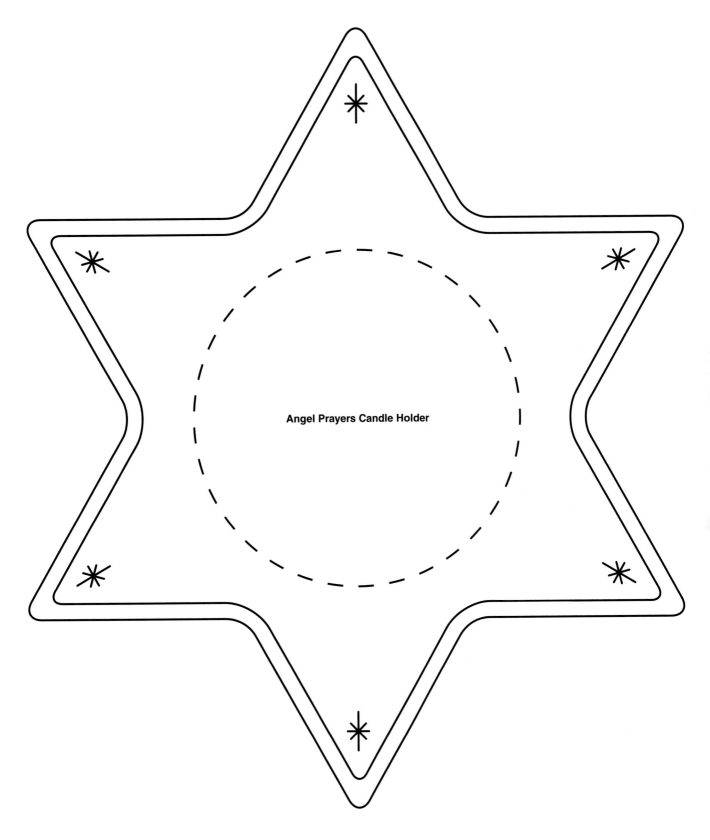

Angel Prayers Candle Holder

Continued on page 84

Angel Prayers Candle Set

*Continued
from page 83*

Angel Prayers Candle

until smooth; remove excess dust with tack cloth. Reproduce pattern and tape in place on plate. Slide black graphite paper under pattern, graphite side down. Using ballpoint pen, trace borderline around star.

2. Base-coat inside borderline with black cherry. Base-coat outside borderline with pine green.

3. Transfer star designs onto plate with white graphite paper. Using #0 liner brush, line border and stars with 14K gold.

4. Apply two coats matte interior spray varnish, allowing varnish to dry between coats. ✳

Angel Ornament

Continued from page 59

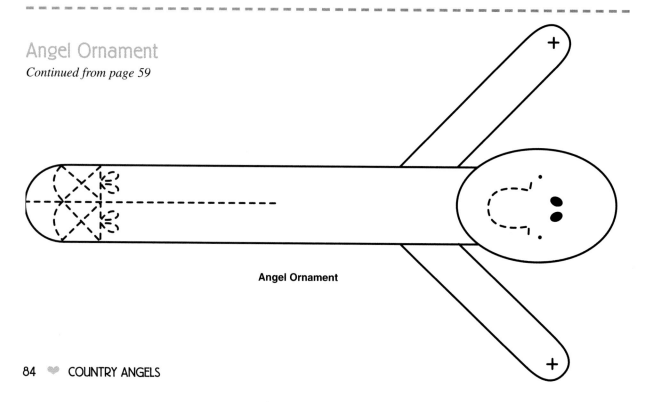

Angel Ornament

Angel Box
Continued from page 57

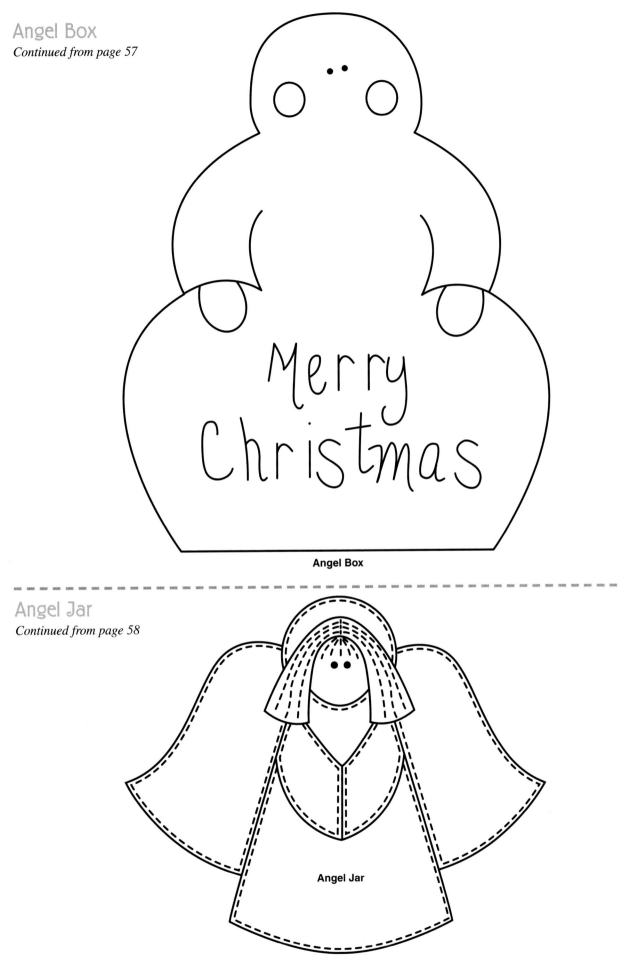

Angel Box

Angel Jar
Continued from page 58

Angel Jar

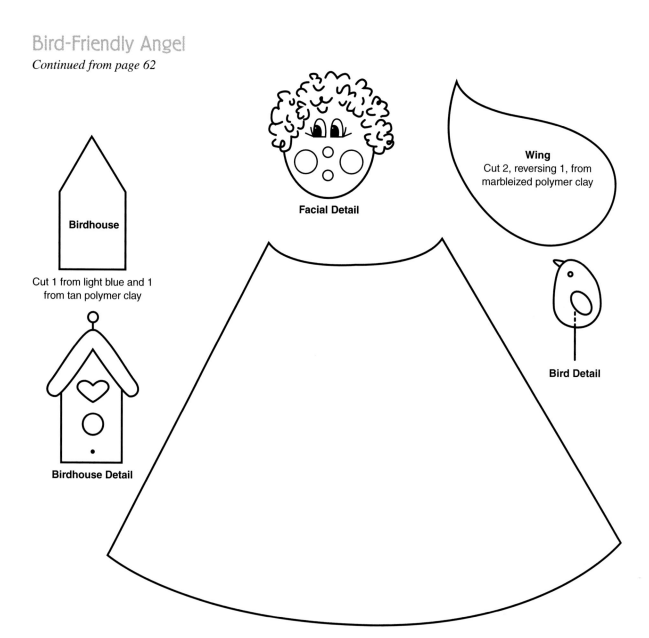

Birdhouse

Cut 1 from light blue and 1
from tan polymer clay

Birdhouse Detail

Facial Detail

Wing
Cut 2, reversing 1, from
marbleized polymer clay

Bird Detail

make dotlike impressions around hole opening. Position birdhouse in angel's right arm as shown; press gently in place.

2. Repeat step 1 to make second birdhouse, using tan for body of birdhouse and red for roof and opening. Using toothpick, poke hole below opening; instead of heart decoration, roll tiny log of brown clay and insert in hole for perch. Insert eye pin into peak of roof.

3. *Bird:* Roll ⅜" ball of red clay into teardrop; form tiny teardrop into wing and press onto side. Pinch yellow clay into a very tiny triangle for beak; press to bird's face. Poke indentation with toothpick for eye. Cut 2" piece of wire; insert one end

½" into bottom of bird and ½" into top of angel's head, allowing a room between the two for gluing on hair later.

4. *Halo:* Shape 1½" circle of wire leaving a 2" tail. Wrap tail twice around point where circle is joined to form halo; twist ends together. Insert tail into top of angel's head, resting halo just beneath bird.

Finishing & Assembly

1. Bake polymer clay figures in 225-degree oven for 20 minutes. Remove baking sheet from oven; allow figures to cool completely before removing them from baking sheet.

2. Using liner brush and black

acrylic paint, outline eyes, paint pupils and add eyelashes. Using white, paint irises and tiny pupil highlights. Let paint dry completely.

3. Spray all polymer clay pieces with one or two coats of glaze, allowing glaze to dry completely between coats.

4. Hot-glue wings to back of angel's dress slightly below shoulders.

5. Glue Spanish moss hair beneath bird and halo, around face and back of head; trim any uneven ends. Glue mini ivy leaves behind bird and below blue birdhouse.

6. Using pliers, join tan and red birdhouse to angel's left hand by attaching jump ring to eye pins. ✳

Continued from page 65

large motif on back of adult's vest.

Tree Skirt

1. Launder fabrics without using fabric softener; dry and press as needed.

2. Following manufacturer's instructions, fuse iron-on adhesive to backs of fabrics. Referring to patterns (pages 88 and 89) and enlarging them as noted in Project Notes, cut appliqués from fabrics:

Cream—five pairs of wings.

Hunter green A—one gown and one pair sleeves from each of two prints A; nine mini trees (skirt trim) from one of the hunter green prints A.

Hunter green B—six mini trees (skirt trim).

Burgundy prints—one gown and one pair sleeves from each of three prints; four mini hearts (skirt trim) from one of the prints.

Flesh-tone fabric—five heads and 10 hands.

Blue check or print—11 stars.

Gold print—three moons and six mini hearts (skirt trim).

3. Remove paper backing from appliqués and arrange on tree skirt as shown, alternating angels with hunter green and burgundy gowns. For skirt trim on burgundy gowns, alternate two gold hearts with three mini trees cut from hunter green A; for trim on hunter green A gowns, alternate two burgundy hearts with three mini trees cut from contrasting hunter green B.

4. Cover design area with pressing

paper and fuse with iron.

5. Glue five ⅜" buttons over top of each angel's head. Glue ½" button to center of each mini heart.

6. Dot on eyes and add smiles with black fabric marking pen. Blush cheeks with cotton swab and cosmetic blusher.

7. Cute jute twine into five 8" and 11 5" pieces; tie each piece in a bow. Glue larger bow to each angel's neckline; glue smaller bow to center of each star.

Adult's Vest

1. Launder vest and fabrics without using fabric softener; dry and press as needed.

2. Referring to patterns (pages 87–89) and enlarging them as noted in Project Notes, cut appliqués from fabrics:

Light gold print—one pair enlarged wings, three enlarged stars and two enlarged mini hearts (skirt trim); one pair wings, four stars and two mini hearts.

Dark gold print—one enlarged moon and one regular moon.

Burgundy print A—one enlarged gown and one enlarged pair of sleeves; one gown and one pair sleeves.

Burgundy print B—six Christmas tree hearts.

Hunter green print—three enlarged mini trees (skirt trim); three mini trees and one Christmas tree.

Flesh-tone fabric—one enlarged head

and one pair enlarged hands; one head and one pair of hands.

3. Remove paper backing from appliqués and arrange on vest, positioning enlarged angel, stars and moon on back of vest; regular angel with three stars and moon on one vest front; and Christmas tree with mini hearts and star on other vest front. Following manufacturer's instructions, fuse appliqués in place.

4. Cut fabric stabilizer to fit inside fronts and back of vest; pin or baste to secure. Using matching rayon embroidery threads for top thread and regular threads in bobbin, machine-appliqué around pieces, beginning with those that appear to be in the back of the design and working forward. Remove fabric stabilizer; trim threads.

5. Sew three buttons over top of angel's head on front; sew five buttons over angel's head on back. Dot on eyes and add smiles to both angels with black fabric marking pen. Blush cheeks with cotton swab and cosmetic blusher.

Child's Vest

1. Follow steps 1 and 2 for adult's vest, cutting appliqués as follows:

Light gold print—one pair wings, four stars and two mini hearts (skirt trim).

Dark gold print—one moon.

Burgundy print A—one gown and one pair of sleeves.

Hunter green print—three mini trees (skirt trim).

Flesh-tone fabric—one head and one pair hands.

2. Refer to steps 3 and 4 for adult's vest, fusing angel, moon and star on one vest front and remaining stars on other vest front.

3. Refer to step 5 for adult's vest, sewing five buttons over top of angel's head and adding face. ❄

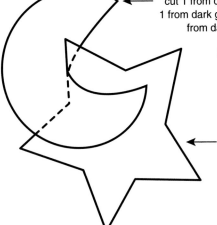

Moon
Cut 3 from gold for tree skirt;
cut 1 from dark gold for adult vest back,
1 from dark gold for adult vest front, and 1
from dark gold for child's vest.

Enlarge patterns for tree skirt
and adult vest back to 155%
before cutting.

Star
Cut 11 from blue print for tree skirt;
from light gold print, cut 3 for adult
vest back, 4 for adult vest front, and
4 for child's vest.

Patterns on page 88

Enlarge patterns for tree skirt
and adult vest back to 155%
before cutting.

Head
From flesh-tone fabric, cut 5
for tree skirt, 1 for adult vest back,
1 for adult vest front, and 1 for child's vest.

Hand
From flesh-tone fabric,
cut 10 for tree skirt, 2 for adult
vest front, and 4 for child's vest.

Sleeve
For tree skirt, cut 1 pair from
each of 2 hunter greens A and
1 pair from each of 3
burgundy prints.

For adult vest, cut 1 pair for
back and 1 pair for front from
burgundy print A.

For child's vest, cut 1 pair from
burgundy print A.

Gown
For tree skirt, cut 1 from each
of 2 hunter greens A and 1 from
each of 3 burgundy prints.

For adult vest, from burgundy,
cut 1 for back and 1 for front.

For child's vest, cut 1 from burgundy.

Wings
Cut 5 from cream for tre
skirt; cut 1 from light go
for adult vest back;
cut 1 from light gold fo
adult vest front and 1 fro
light gold for child's vest.

Mini Tree
For tree skirt, cut 9 from one
hunter green A and 6 from
hunter green B.

For adult's vest, from hunter
green, cut 3 for back
and 3 for front.

For child's vest, cut 3
from hunter green.

Mini Heart
For tree skirt, cut 4 from
burgundy and 6 from gold.

For adult vest, cut 2 from light
gold for back, and 2 from
light gold for fronts.

For child's vest, cut 2
from light gold print.

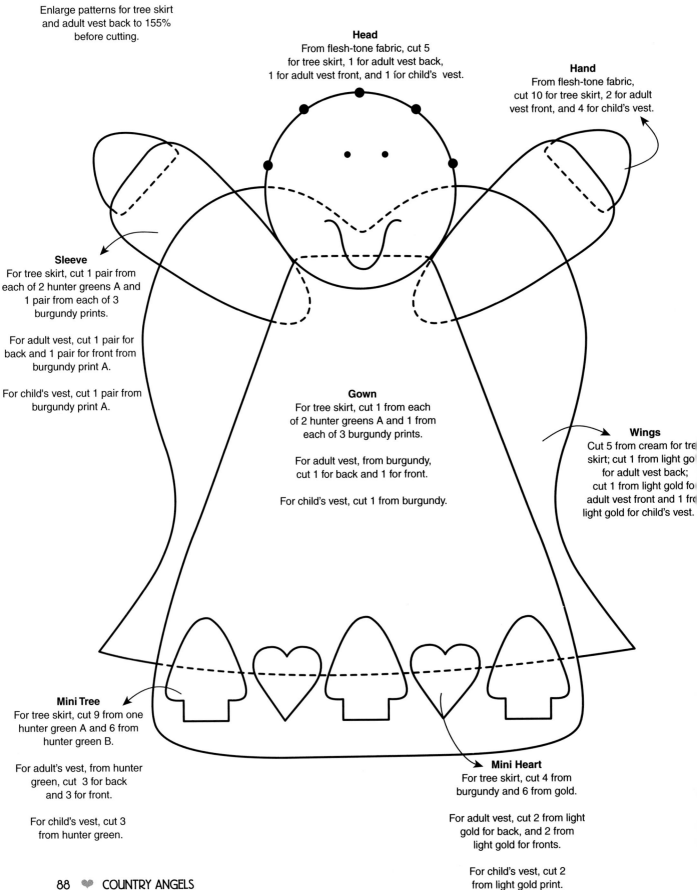

Jute Angel Tree Skirt & Denim Vests

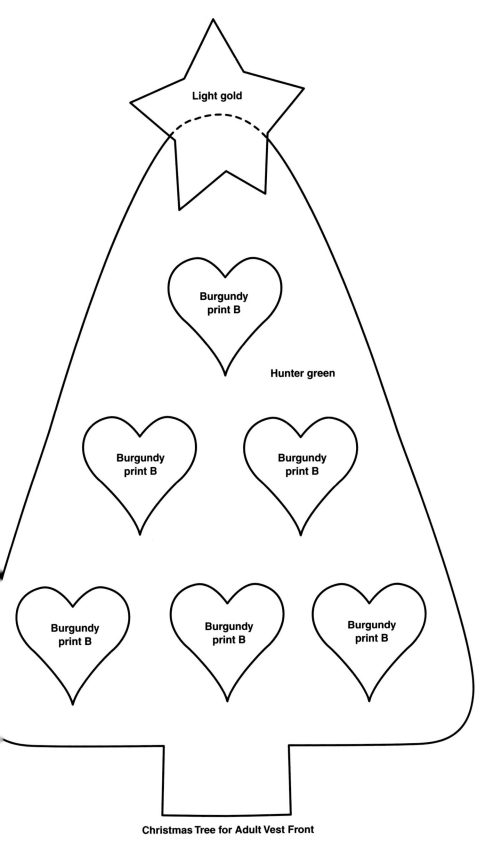

Light gold

Burgundy print B

Hunter green

Burgundy print B

Burgundy print B

Burgundy print B

Burgundy print B

Burgundy print B

Christmas Tree for Adult Vest Front

"Life Is Fragile" Wall Hanging

Continued from page 63

and join tapered ends to dress neckline, draping sleeves toward center front of dress.

2. Cut two wings from rolled white polymer clay and join one to each side of body beneath arms.

Assembly & Finishing

1. Cut six stars from rolled gold polymer clay. Place a star between each angel's hands and set others aside on baking sheet.

2. Bake polymer clay figures in a 225-degree oven for 10 minutes. Remove baking sheet from oven; allow polymer clay figures to cool completely before removing them from baking sheet.

3. Using liner brush and black acrylic paint, outline eyes, paint pupils and add eyelashes. Using white, paint irises and tiny pupil highlights. Using red, paint angels' mouths.

4. Paint white lettering on plaque. Dip tip of paintbrush handle in white paint and dot paint on ends of letters. Let all paints dry completely.

5. Spray all polymer clay pieces with one or two coats of glaze, allowing glaze to dry completely between coats.

6. Hot-glue angels and stars to plaque as shown. Fray edges of fabric strip; tie in bow and glue to plaque, near edge and below green angel. ✳

Patterns on page 92

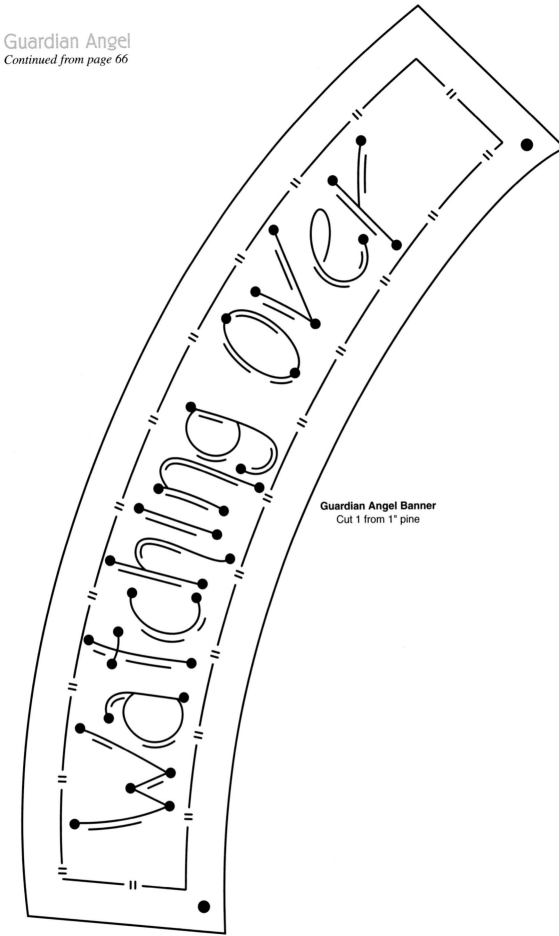

Guardian Angel Banner
Cut 1 from 1" pine

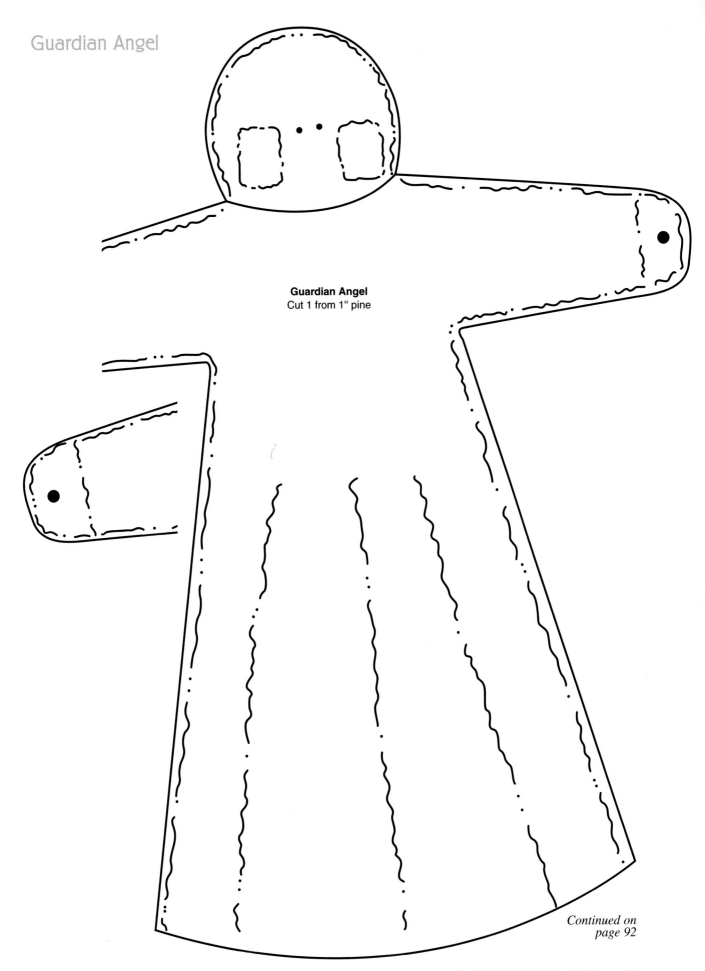

Guardian Angel
Cut 1 from 1" pine

Continued on page 92

Guardian Angel
Continued from page 91

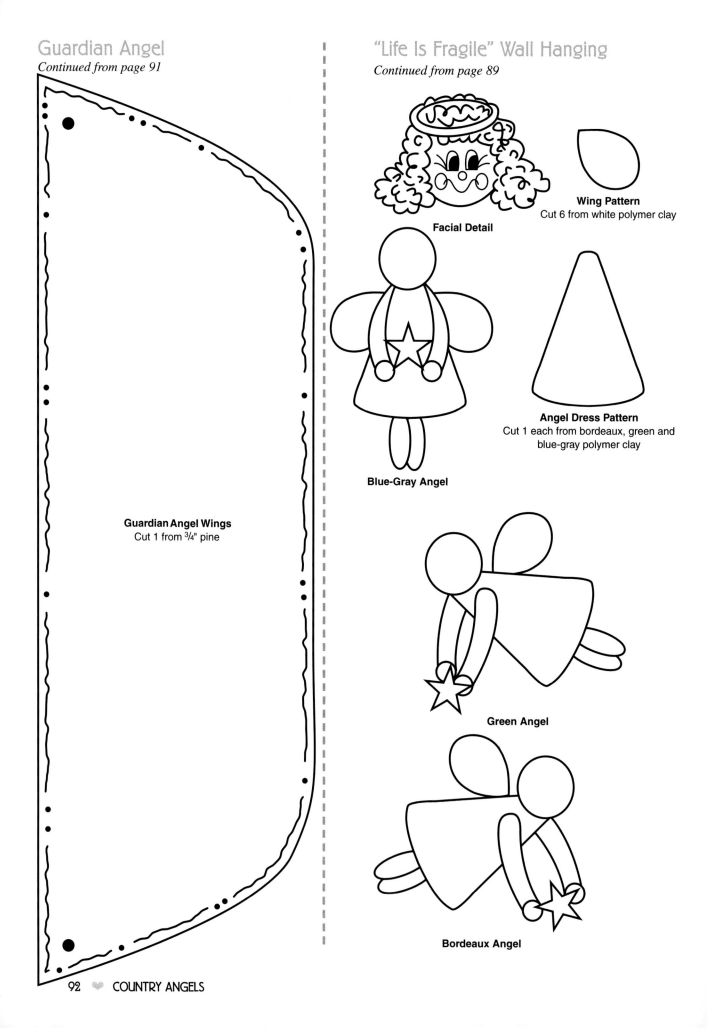

Guardian Angel Wings
Cut 1 from ³⁄₄" pine

"Life Is Fragile" Wall Hanging
Continued from page 89

Facial Detail

Wing Pattern
Cut 6 from white polymer clay

Blue-Gray Angel

Angel Dress Pattern
Cut 1 each from bordeaux, green and
blue-gray polymer clay

Green Angel

Bordeaux Angel

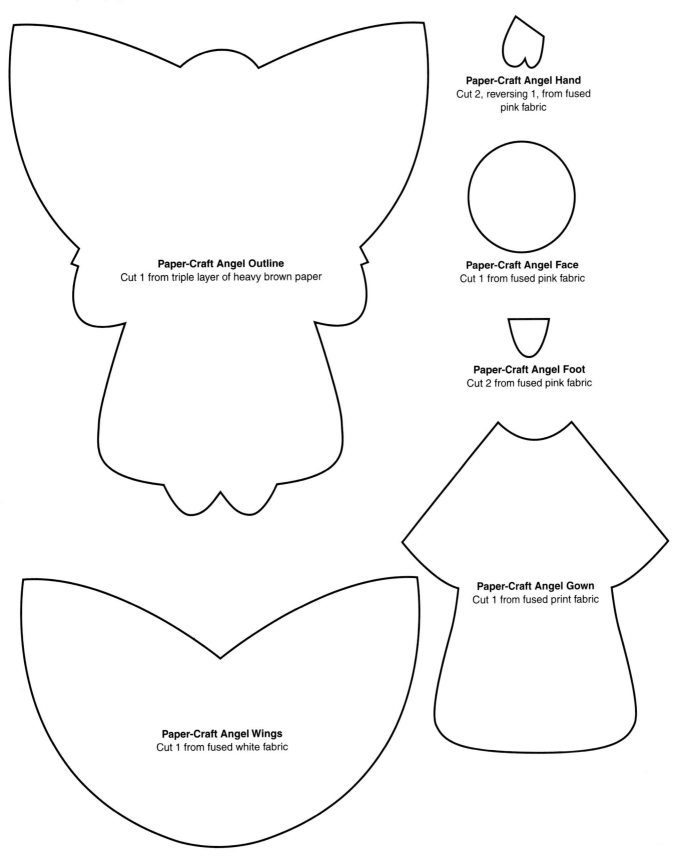

Paper-Craft Angel Hand
Cut 2, reversing 1, from fused pink fabric

Paper-Craft Angel Outline
Cut 1 from triple layer of heavy brown paper

Paper-Craft Angel Face
Cut 1 from fused pink fabric

Paper-Craft Angel Foot
Cut 2 from fused pink fabric

Paper-Craft Angel Gown
Cut 1 from fused print fabric

Paper-Craft Angel Wings
Cut 1 from fused white fabric

Christmas Angel Tree Topper

Continued from page 70

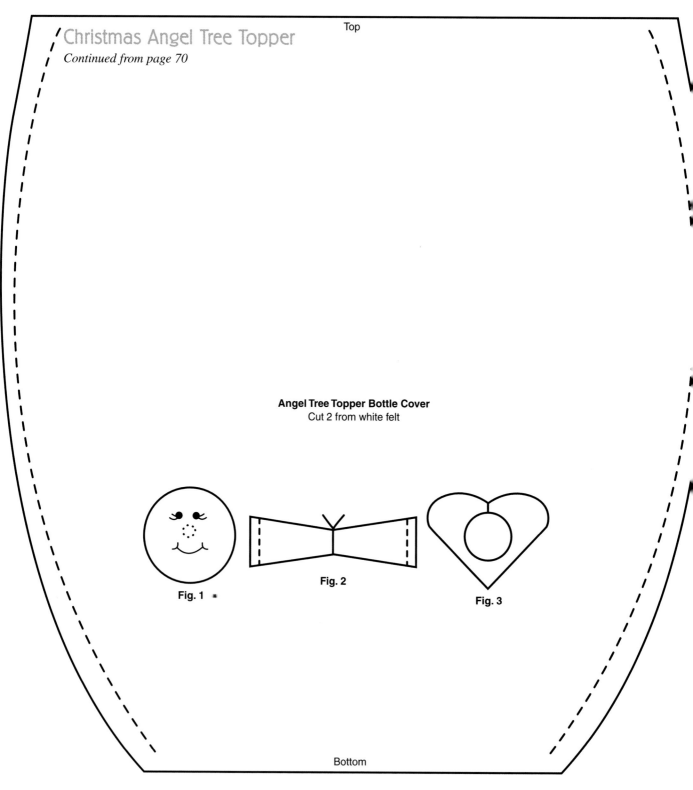

Top

Angel Tree Topper Bottle Cover
Cut 2 from white felt

Fig. 1

Fig. 2

Fig. 3

Bottom

around each arm just above lace; pull gathers tight to close arm and enclose stuffing; knot thread. Glue center of arms to back of dress at neck.

5. *Collar:* Referring to Fig. 3, cut 1½" circle from Battenburg heart; clip slit from center top of heart to opening. Glue doily around bottleneck with opening in back.

Finishing

1. Cut several 3" strands of doll hair; twist together in center and glue at top of head. Arrange curls as desired, adding more hair around face and filling back; spot-glue hair as needed to hold it in place.

2. For halo, wrap star garland

around four fingers; slip off fingers and twist ends together to hold shape. Glue to top of head. Glue gold satin heart to front of halo.

3. Tie ribbon into bow; glue to center front of angel at neckline. Glue wings to back of dress.

4. Loop string of Christmas tree lights over hands; spot-glue to hold. ✳

Gingerbread Angel Apron

Continued from page 72

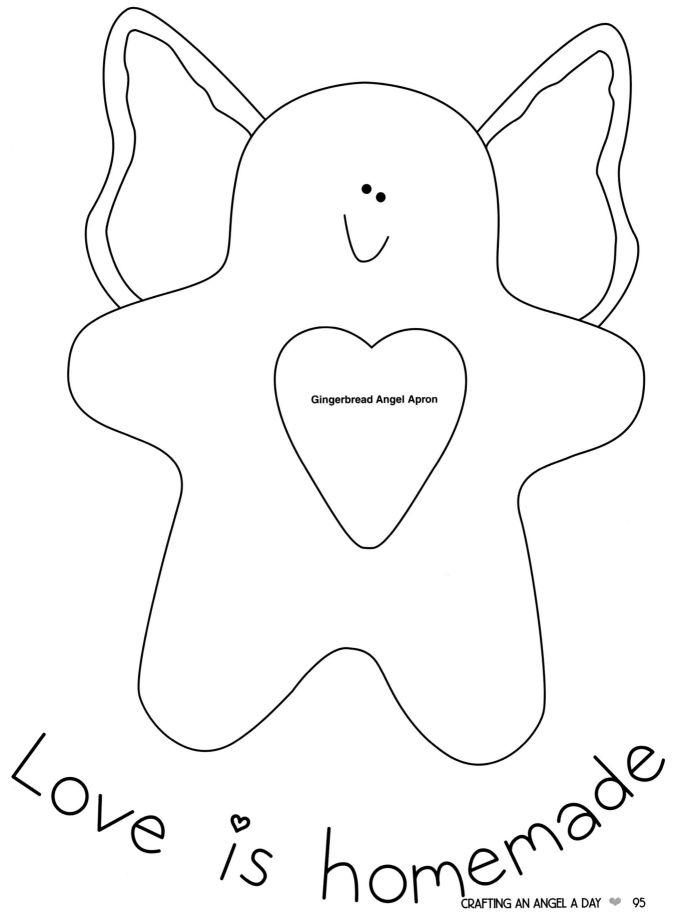

Gingerbread Angel Apron

Love is homemade

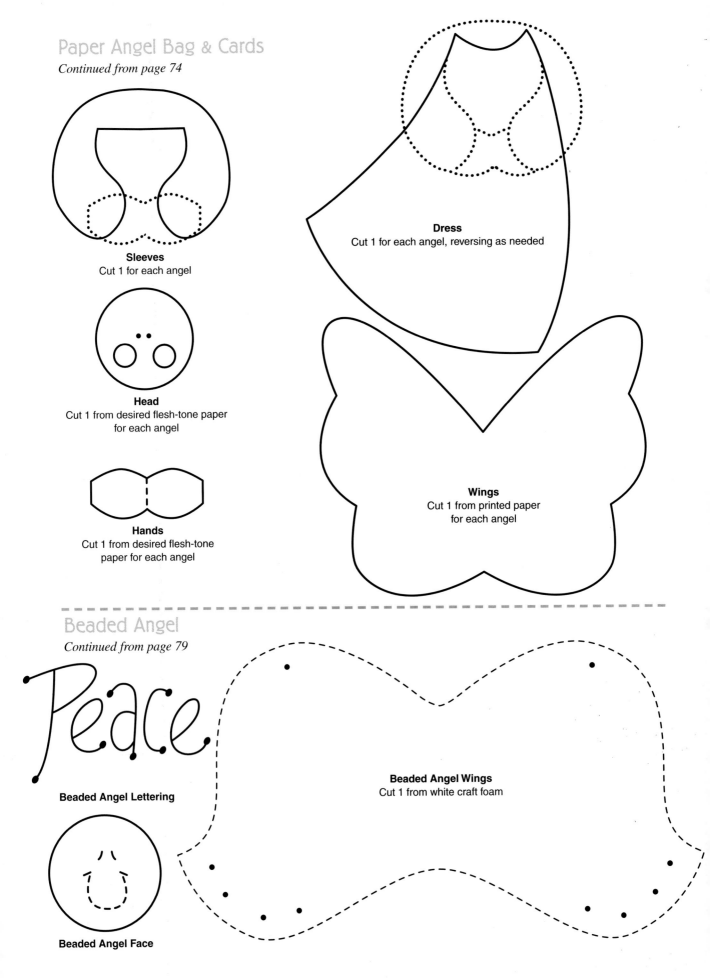

Paper Angel Bag & Cards
Continued from page 74

Sleeves
Cut 1 for each angel

Head
Cut 1 from desired flesh-tone paper
for each angel

Hands
Cut 1 from desired flesh-tone
paper for each angel

Dress
Cut 1 for each angel, reversing as needed

Wings
Cut 1 from printed paper
for each angel

Beaded Angel
Continued from page 79

Peace

Beaded Angel Lettering

Beaded Angel Face

Beaded Angel Wings
Cut 1 from white craft foam

Angel with Heart Basket

Continued from page 75

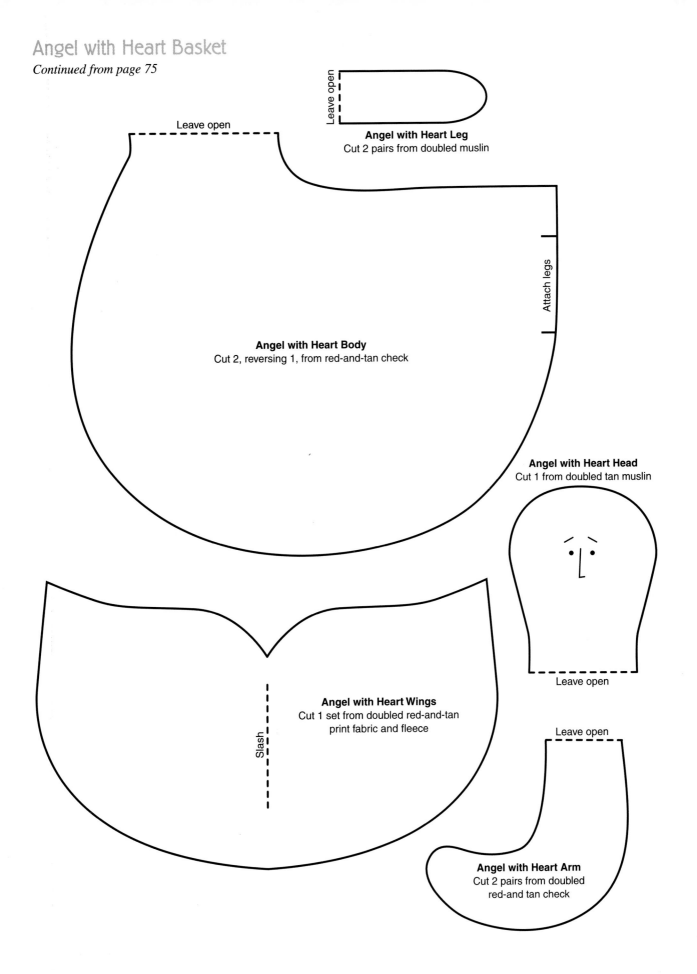

Leave open

Angel with Heart Leg
Cut 2 pairs from doubled muslin

Leave open

Attach legs

Angel with Heart Body
Cut 2, reversing 1, from red-and-tan check

Angel with Heart Head
Cut 1 from doubled tan muslin

Leave open

Angel with Heart Wings
Cut 1 set from doubled red-and-tan
print fabric and fleece

Slash

Leave open

Angel with Heart Arm
Cut 2 pairs from doubled
red-and tan check

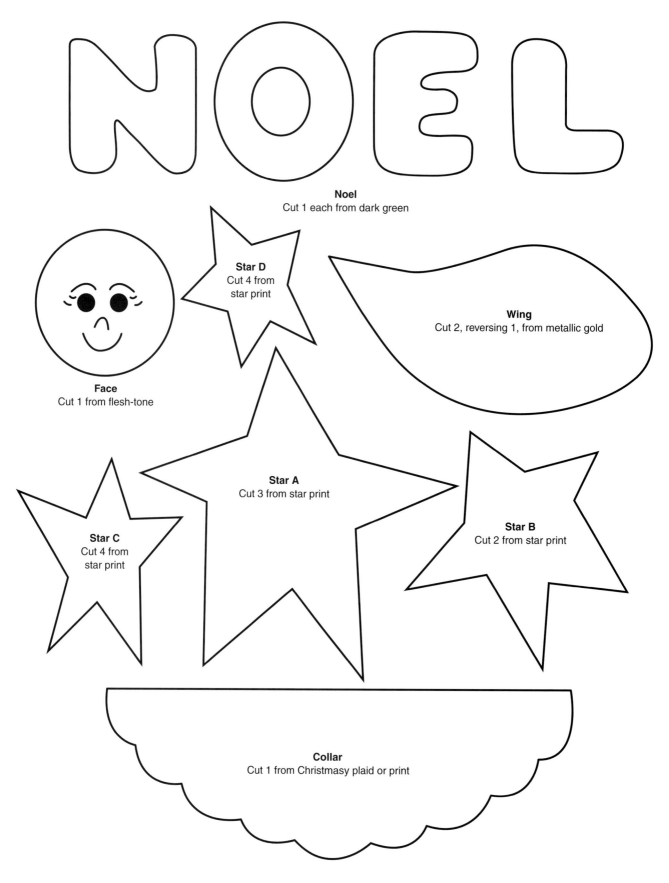

Noel
Cut 1 each from dark green

Star D
Cut 4 from
star print

Wing
Cut 2, reversing 1, from metallic gold

Face
Cut 1 from flesh-tone

Star A
Cut 3 from star print

Star B
Cut 2 from star print

Star C
Cut 4 from
star print

Collar
Cut 1 from Christmasy plaid or print

COLOR KEY
B Blue
L Light blue
BL Black
W White
R Red
P Pink
Y Yellow
G Gold

Snowflakes on your nose are an angel's happy Kisses.

Angel Kisses Pie Tin

F rom elegant angels to cute-as-a-button angels, this collection of Victorian-style crafts will add an enchanting touch to your home!

Victorian
ANGELS

With her pure white feathered wings rising behind her, and dressed in ecru lace accented with ribbons and a rose, this angel makes an elegant decoration.

Rosebud Angel

Design by Marie Le Fevre

Materials
- 2½" porcelain angel head with hands
- 4 (4"–6") white feathers
- Lace fabric:
  ½ yard for dress
  3" x 6" to enclose batting
- 2 yrds matching (1"-wide) ruffled lace
- 1½ yards (⅛"-wide) ecru satin ribbon
- Craft batting:
  2" x 5" strip
  5" square
- 12" white chenille stem
- 2 peach ribbon roses with leaves
- Hot-glue gun
- Hand-sewing needle and matching thread
- Straight pins
- Rubber band

Project Notes
Refer to photo throughout.

Enlarge pattern for skirt 125 and train 200 percent before tracing or cutting out.

Doll
Note: It is important to wrap batting and fabric as tightly as possible, as it must fit into opening in doll's head.

1. For body, fold 5" square of batting into thirds, then fold in half; bundle will measure about 2½" x 1⅔". Wrap thread around middle of batting or apply glue to secure.

2. Wrap 3" x 6" lace fabric around batting, folding edges under. Pull fabric tightly, stitching ends together.

3. Cut chenille stem in half; fold each piece in half.

4. Cut 2" x 5" batting into two 2" x 2½" pieces. Wrap each piece around a folded chenille stem; glue in place. Apply glue to one end of each stem and insert about ½" of stem into doll arms; let dry.

Dress & Assembly
1. Referring to patterns (page 123), cut sleeves, skirt and train from lace fabric.

2. Sew or glue ruffled lace around edges of skirt, and along sides and around point of train; sew or glue additional ruffled lace along 2" edge of each sleeve.

3. Fold sleeves in half lengthwise with ruffled lace at cuffs; sew or glue seams. Slip chenille stem with arm into sleeves. Adjust hands so they show as desired. Trim fabric to length of chenille stem; glue together.

4. Drape skirt over body; adjust fabric so back of skirt hangs 3" lower than front of skirt. Form pleats at top so fabric drapes evenly.

5. Drape train over skirt and body; adjust so back point of train hangs 3" lower than back of skirt.

6. Gather fabric and body tightly to fit into body; wrap tightly with a rubber band to secure.

7. Before gluing body to head, check to see that fabric drapes properly and that gathered end will fit in opening.

8. Glue body and fabric into opening in doll head. Glue arms into doll head opening on each side of body, making sure hands are correctly positioned.

Finishing
1. Cut 18" piece of ribbon; fold in half and knot each end. Attach to center back of doll near bottom of shoulder, first gluing knots to fabric and then gluing ribbon strands up back of doll to base of hair. This creates a secure hanger.

2. Cut an 8" piece of ruffled lace. Run gathering stitch through top edge and gather gently to fit around shoulders in a V-shaped neckline; glue in place.

3. Glue feathers at center back over lace and hanger.

4. Glue one ribbon rose to center back of angel where feathered wings meet.

5. Fold 1 yard of ribbon in half; tie in overhand knot bow with 2" loops; streamers should be as long as angel's gown. Glue ribbon to center front of lace collar and glue remaining ribbon rose to center of bow. ✳

Patterns on page 123

K

eep your most treasured jewelry inside this decorative bureau box to make a pretty and practical accent.

Keepsake Box

Design by Judy Atwell

Materials
- 6"-diameter round papier-mâché box with lid
- Pearl finish #02 601 Ceramcoat Gleams acrylic paint from Delta Technical Coatings Inc.
- Flat paintbrush
- Small piece of sponge
- 2 (12") white chenille stems
- 2 (12") squares metallic gold tissue lamé
- Matching thread and hand-sewing needle
- 20" square white tulle
- 1¾" flat-back porcelain lady head
- 2 (3") strands 2mm iridecent pearls
- 2 (4") strands 4mm white pearls
- 7 (¼") metallic gold ribbon roses
- 7" x 4" lace trim
- Pink crystal fine glitter
- Clear-drying white craft glue
- Small disposable foam paintbrush
- Aluminum foil
- Wire cutters
- Hot-glue gun

Project Notes
Refer to photo throughout.

Use hot glue for all assembly; white glue is used only for glitter.

Painting Box
1. Cover work surface with aluminum foil. Remove lid from box; set both pieces upside down on foil. Base-coat all exterior surfaces of lid and box with pearl acrylic paint; let dry. Apply a second coat; let dry.

2. Squeeze a puddle of pearl paint onto corner of foil; using sponge, daub a heavy third coat of paint onto all painted surfaces for added texture. Let dry.

Wings
1. Twist together ends of one chenille stem to make a loop; hold twist so it will remain at center and side of wing. With fingers, bend loop into a wing shape. Repeat with

second chenille stem (twists will join at center back).

2. Thread needle and have it at hand. Fold one square of lamé over one chenille wing, corner to corner, holding gathers of lamé at the twist with one hand and using the other to gather up all the lamé at the twist as you mold it to the chenille frame.

3. With needle and thread, sew lamé gathers securely in place; wrap thread tightly around gathered fabric at twist. Make sure you catch all edges; sew through them once again and knot thread. Trim off excess lamé and set wing aside. Repeat with remaining lamé and wing frame.

Assembly
1. From corner of tulle, cut a circle at least 1" larger than lid. Gather

circle in the center; apply a blob of glue to the center of the lid and push the gathers into glue, leaving edges of tulle free.

2. Glue wings together on top of this center spot. Glue them to box only at centers, leaving rest of wings free.

3. Cut 2" x 12" strip of tulle; twist the entire length until it starts to coil. Form coil tightly to fit angel's head and glue directly over her hair. Glue two lengths of iridescent pearls in loops over the tulle, draping them partly over her hair, positioning all ends of pearl strands behind the sides of her head. Glue on one strand of white pearls in the same manner.

4. Cut 6" square of tulle; gather it in a pouf and glue to the back of head with pouf showing 1"–1½" at top. Glue porcelain head to box between wings.

5. Snip stems from ribbon roses using wire cutters. Glue two at top right of head and three at bottom left; reserve other two for now.

6. Turn under ends of lace 1"; stitch with needle and thread. Turn bottom edge under almost in half. Glue center of top edge under center of angel's face. Continue gluing each side of top around face, slightly overlapping wings. Pouf bottom fold to fit space; adjust as desired and glue.

7. Glue remaining pearls around neckline, concealing ends in folds of lace. Glue two roses at neckline over one end of pearls.

8. With disposable foam brush, lightly brush white glue on tulle head wrap in a few spots, and on edges of neck pouf and deep into folds of lamé wings. Sprinkle with glitter; let dry and shake off excess. ✳

Dress up your wardrobe throughout the year with this charming little angel pin!

Golden Angel Pin

Design by Chris Malone

Materials
- ♥ 4" wooden mustache/wings cutout
- ♥ 1" round wooden plug
- ♥ 1½" piece dark blond Beautiful Braids crepe mohair doll hair from One & Only Creations
- ♥ 9" piece gold 24-gauge wire
- ♥ 14" piece (⅜"-wide) metallic gold wire-edge ribbon
- ♥ Brass charms:
  ⅞" star
  1" heart
- ♥ Acrylic paints: white, black, desired flesh tone, and darker flesh tone for shading
- ♥ Small flat paintbrush
- ♥ Small stencil brush
- ♥ Toothpick
- ♥ Satin varnish
- ♥ 1" brass pin back
- ♥ Hand-sewing needle and thread
- ♥ Paper towel
- ♥ Hot-glue gun

Project Notes
Refer to photo throughout.

Let all paints and varnish dry between coats and applications.

Instructions
1. Base-coat wings with two coats white paint; base-coat wooden plug with flesh-tone paint.

2. Dot eyes onto rounded surface of plug with tip of paintbrush handle dipped in black paint.

3. Dip stencil brush into darker flesh tone; remove most of paint on paper towel and tap nearly dry brush to cheeks to "blush" them. Using tip of toothpick, add white highlight dot to each cheek.

4. Brush wings and face with satin varnish.

5. Glue head to center of wings. Apply glue to top of head and wrap a length of doll hair all around top of head, beginning in the back.

6. For halo, coil wire several times around pencil. Slip off pencil and pull coils apart slightly to shape coiled wire in an arc. Apply glue to each end of wire and poke into hair at sides, gluing halo to head.

7. Apply glue to one tip of brass star charm; poke into hair to glue to head.

8. Tie gold ribbon in a bow. Tie a knot in each end; trim ends at an angle. Sew charm to center bottom of bow, stitching through charm's hanging loop. Glue bow to bottom of head.

9. Glue pin back to back of wings. ✳

T

ransform scraps of lace and doilies into treasured heirloom ornaments!

Victorian Lace Angel

Design by Kathleen George

Materials

- ♥ 4"-tall Styrofoam cone
- ♥ 1½" Styrofoam ball
- ♥ 12" square cream velveteen fabric
- ♥ Assorted lace motifs and doilies
- ♥ Fabric stiffener
- ♥ Doll curls
- ♥ 2 straight pins with black ball heads
- ♥ 24" (⅛"-wide) cream ribbon
- ♥ ½" craft pins
- ♥ White tacky glue
- ♥ Hot-glue gun

Project Note

Refer to photo throughout.

Instructions

1. Hot-glue foam ball to top of cone.

2. Referring to pattern (page 124), cut velveteen fabric to cover cone; pin or glue velveteen to cone. Trim excess velveteen from bottom, leaving ½" excess; fold excess smoothly onto bottom of foam cone.

3. Cut 2" circle of velveteen; glue to base of cone, covering velveteen edges. Cut 1¼" circle of velveteen; glue over face area on foam ball.

4. Cut heavy lace motif into two wing shapes approximately 4" across. Stiffen according to directions on stiffener bottle; set aside to dry.

5. Cover cone with a doily that has a decorative edge, positioning edge at bottom so it extends beyond bottom of cone. Pin or glue doily in place at back of cone.

6. Glue strip of lace around neck, covering edge of doily.

7. Cut two 4" x 2" pieces of doily; fold in half to make 2" squares. Glue to sides for arms (fold should be at top of arm), placing arms at an angle with top front corners close together. Glue small lace floral motif to front of cone where arms meet. Tie 8" piece of ribbon in bow; glue or pin in center of floral motif.

8. Glue doll curls to head, covering all areas not covered by velveteen. Push pins with black heads into head for eyes.

9. Push hanging loop of remaining ribbon into top of head; secure with glue. Pin or glue wings to center back of angel. ✳

Pattern on page 124

D

ress up your Christmas tree with this lovely little lady! Layers of ruffles accented with glittery paint and golden jingle bells make her outfit extra special!

Teardrop Angel Ornament

Design by Veleta Stafney

Materials

- Plastic 130mm crystal teardrop ornament
- Shredded gold metallic Mylar
- 9" fine gold cord
- 1" wooden furniture button
- 2 (¾" x 1") wooden spools
- 6" x 2½-yard strip white tulle
- ½ yard (⅝"-wide) iridescent ribbon
- 2 (12mm) gold jingle bells
- Winter white Mini-Curl doll hair from One & Only Creations
- Ceramcoat acrylic paints from Delta Technical Coatings:
  Adobe red #2046
  Medium flesh #2126
  White #2505
  Black #2506
- Ceramcoat satin-finish interior varnish
- Ceramcoat Sparkle Glaze #07 012 from Delta Technical Coatings
- Imitation gold wedding band
- ½ yard (¼"-wide) metallic gold ribbon
- Black fine-point marking pen
- Paintbrush
- Stylus
- Toothpick
- Hand-sewing needle and white thread
- Cotton-tip swabs
- Tacky glue

Project Notes

Refer to photo throughout.

Let all paints and ink dry between coats and applications.

Instructions

1. Separate halves of plastic teardrop; fill with shredded Mylar. Snap teardrop together. Thread gold cord through hanging loop in top of ornament; knot.

2. Paint furniture button and spools medium flesh. Referring to facial detail drawing, dot on eyes using stylus dipped in black paint. Using cotton-tip swab to apply adobe red, lightly blush cheeks. Add nose and eyelashes with fine-point marking pen. Highlight eyes with tiny dots of white paint applied with tip of toothpick.

3. Coat painted head with varnish. Glue head to top of plastic teardrop.

4. Cut off a 1-yard piece of tulle; set aside for wings. Make dress from remaining tulle: For collar, fold over 1½" along one long edge. Sew basting stitch through both layers ¼" from fold. Place strip around head under neck; pull thread ends to gather tulle tightly and evenly. Knot thread.

5. For arms, cut ⅝"-wide iridescent ribbon in half. Wrap half around each spool; glue. Glue gold jingle bell (hand) to end of each spool. Glue flat ends of spools to sides of angel, under collar and over dress.

6. Cut several 3" strands of hair; twist in center and glue to top of head. Add hair to sides and back,

filling in evenly. Trim as needed. Glue wedding band to top of head for halo.

7. For wings, fold remaining 1-yard piece of tulle in half lengthwise; tie in four-loop bow. Fluff and separate loops; glue bow to back of neck.

8. Tie gold ribbon in small bow; glue at angel's neckline. Using cotton-tip swab, apply highlights of sparkle glaze to hair, wings and dress. ❄

Teardrop Angel Facial Detail

Display a favorite portrait inside this stained-glass-style frame to create a family keepsake!

My Guardian Angel Frame

Design by Bonnie Lester

Materials

- 8" x 10" picture frame
- 8" x 10" white picture matte with 5" x 7" oval opening
- Treasure Gold Florentine #3020 wax metallic finish from Plaid Enterprises
- Black #16025 Gallery Glass simulated liquid leading from Plaid Enterprises
- Gallery Glass window colors from Plaid Enterprises:
  Snow white #16002
  Cameo ivory #16003
  Sunny yellow #16004
  Canyon coral #16006
  Emerald green #16009
  Royal blue #16012
  Ruby red #16015
- Toothpicks
- Tape
- Window cleaner
- Paper towels
- Paper clip
- Soft cloth
- Single-edge razor blade or craft knife

Project Notes

Refer to photo throughout.

Using photocopier with enlarging capabilities, enlarge pattern (page 125) to 125 percent.

Working with Liquid Leading

To apply leading, apply firm, even pressure on bottle. Keep tip above work, allowing an even "rope" of leading to fall in place over pattern lines. To end a line, gently touch tip to glass and release pressure on bottle at the same time. Where leading has spread too wide or run together, allow leading to stand for about 10 minutes, and then gently reshape leading with a toothpick.

Tips for Working with Window Colors

Touch tip to glass and apply gentle, even pressure to release paint. For large areas, move tip back and forth in the same direction, as you would color a picture. Push paint into tight areas and corners with a toothpick.

To avoid bubbles, raise tip before releasing pressure. Remove large bubbles by touching them with a fingertip; deflate small bubbles with a toothpick.

Leading

1. Clean glass from picture frame with window cleaner and soft cloth to remove dust and fingerprints; let dry. Place glass directly over pattern (page 125). Secure pattern to glass at opposite corners, using small amounts of tape and taking care not to cover any lines on pattern.

2. Remove tip from liquid leading bottle; remove cap from tip. Poke small hole in cap with paper clip. Remove seal covering leading and replace tip. Replace cap.

3. Hold bottle upside down. Shake leading into tip with short, firm motions (like you are shaking down a thermometer). It is important to keep the tip full of leading at all times to avoid air bubbles.

4. Referring to "Working with Liquid Leading", outline design in the following order, being careful not to apply leading to arrows:

- Angel face, eyes, chin, hair and halo;
- Center oval, starting at rose and working clockwise around pattern;
- Wings;
- Roses and leaves, following direction of arrows on pattern; start at top right and work clockwise around pattern;
- Vine and outer oval, starting at top left and working counterclockwise around pattern;
- Remaining lines—horizontal, diagonal from center out, and outer rectangle.

5. Allow leading to dry undisturbed for at least 2 hours.

Window Color

1. Carefully follow manufacturer's instructions to prepare window color. Gently shake paint down from tip before removing lid.

2. Referring to "Working with Window Colors", apply glass paint in the following order:

- *Face*—canyon coral;
- *Hair*—sunny yellow;
- *Wings and halo*—snow white;
- *Roses*—ruby red;
- *Leaves*—emerald green;
- *Oval frame*—cameo ivory;
- *Background frame*—royal blue.

3. Let painted glass dry on a flat, level surface overnight; do not move project for at least 8 hours.

Finishing

1. When glass is completely dry, apply wax metallic finish to all leaded areas, rubbing gently in crosswise direction.

2. Place glass in frame; place matte behind glass; add picture of your choice. ✳

Pattern on page 125

Craft this pair of diminutive angels from scraps in just a few minutes!

Liberty Bell Angels

Design by Ann Butler

Project Note
Refer to photo throughout.

Instructions
1. Thread a 6" piece of fine wire through top edge of longer lace strip; twist wire ends together to form a circle of tightly gathered lace.

2. Bend down top loop on bell; glue gathered wire lace atop bell. (Lace drapes down over bell to form angel's skirt.)

3. Fold metallic thread or floss in half; knot ends together. Slip looped end through pearl bead and pull all the way through (loop will extend from top of angel's pearl "head" to form hanger). Glue bead with knotted thread at

Materials
Larger Gold Angel
- 1" gold bell
- ⅝" pearl bead
- 3" gold tinsel stem
- 8" metallic gold thread or embroidery floss
- 1¾"-wide gold metallic lace: 13" and 18" pieces

Smaller Silver Angel
- ⅞" silver bell
- ½" pearl bead
- 3" silver tinsel stem
- 8" metallic silver thread or embroidery floss
- 1¼"-wide silver metallic lace: 12" and 14" pieces

Each Angel
- Fine craft wire
- Hand-sewing needle
- Hot-glue gun

bottom on top of lace-topped bell.

4. Bend tinsel stem into ½"-diameter halo; bend ends straight down. Glue halo stem to back of head bead so halo rests about ¼" above head.

5. For wings, repeat step 1 with remaining lace and wire. Glue lace circle upright to back of angel to form wings. ✲

Dig through your collection of beads and buttons to create this charming little pin!

Miniature Heart Pin

Design by E. Wayne Fox

Project Notes
Refer to photo throughout.

Instructions
1. For wings, open jump ring; thread leaves back to back on jump ring;

Materials
- 15mm x 13mm gold filigree heart bead
- 8mm ivory pearl bead
- 2 (15mm x 10mm) gold metal dogwood leaf charms
- 6mm gold jump ring
- 2" (20-gauge) gold craft wire
- ¾" gold pin back
- Round-nose pliers
- Wire cutters
- Aleene's Platinum Bond adhesive

close jump ring.

2. Referring to Fig. 1, bend wire for halo. Using round-nose pliers, roll ½" section at top into oval as shown. Thread both ends of wire through

Fig. 1

same end of pearl bead (head).

3. Thread long wire end through jump ring and from bottom (point) to top through the heart bead (body).

4. Adjust angel so halo is at front and wings are at back. Bend wire to back and trim. Glue pin back to back of angel. ✲

F

olded paper dressed up with paper cutouts and charms becomes keepsake gift boxes sure to be treasured!

Keepsake Gift Boxes

Design by Sandra Graham Smith

Materials
- 8½" x 11" piece colored cardstock
- Stylus or dry ballpoint pen
- Embroidery floss in coordinating color
- Tacky glue
- Gift wrap or other decorative paper
- Paper doily
- Assorted stickers
- Silver snowflakes cut from silver snowflake garland and/or other decorative charms, buttons, beads, etc.
- Decorative paper edgers

Project Note
Refer to photo throughout.

Instructions
1. Referring to pattern (page 126), trace one onto card stock; cut out. Using ruler and stylus, score all dotted lines.

2. Bend box together, gluing tab only to adjacent side. Tie floss into a hanging loop; glue knot as shown by dot on pattern. Let glue dry thoroughly.

3. Decorate three sides of box as desired with decorative designs cut from wrapping paper or decorative paper and/or snowflake designs from paper doilies. Add stickers, buttons, charms, beads, etc., as desired. ✳

Pattern on page 126

B

eautiful burgundy and gold satins drape around this peaceful Christmas angel.

Victorian Treetop Angel

Design by Bonnie Lester

Materials

- Doll parts from Fibre Craft:
  2½" porcelain doll head #7689
  1⅝" porcelain doll hands #7693
- 6¾" acrylic doll cone
- 4 (12") white 6mm chenille stems
- ⅔ yard burgundy crepe-backed satin
- ½ yard matching tulle
- ½ yard gold lamé
- ½ yard ¼" metallic gold braided trim
- 24-gauge gold beading wire #BWG-24 from Crafts Etc.!
- 2 (1") gold metallic bows
- 1" dove
- 3" feather wings #WFWA-3 from Crafts Etc.!
- Velverette craft glue from Delta Technical Coatings
- Hand-sewing needle and matching threads
- Sewing machine
- Iron
- Low-temperature glue gun
- Loop puller or small safety pin
- Needle-nose pliers
- Wire clippers

Project Notes

Refer to photo throughout.

Use ¼" seam allowance throughout unless otherwise instructed.

Body Assembly

1. Fold one chenille stem in half; twist to form ends. Drop a small amount of hot glue into the hollow of each porcelain hand. Place one hand on each end of twisted stem.

2. Fold second stem in half over center of arms; twist second stem from fold to ends (making a "T.")

3. Attach one end of a third chenille stem to top of "T" using about 1" of stem. Wind remaining 11" of stem around and around top of center post just under arms, forming chest area.

4. Attach upper chenille body to porcelain head/shoulders using a liberal amount of hot glue, applying firm pressure until glue cools and sets.

5. Using craft glue, attach upper body to acrylic cone, gluing end of center post (waist) and placing it inside hole at top of cone. Let dry.

Clothing

1. Referring to patterns (pages 127–129), cut two dresses on fold from satin; cut also one shawl and one halo from satin. From lamé, cut two skirt linings on fold and one shawl. From tulle, cut an 8" x 36" rectangle.

2. *Petticoat:* Fold tulle in half lengthwise. Hand-baste across full 36" raw edge through both thicknesses, pulling thread to gather. Wrap gathered edge around angel's waist; stitch tulle ends together and knot gathering thread to secure.

3. Right sides facing, sew satin dress halves together at shoulders, underarm and side seams. Notch under arms and at waist.

4. Right sides facing, sew lamé skirt lining halves together along side seams; turn right side out.

5. Place skirt lining inside dress, right sides facing and matching side seams. Sew around bottom of skirt. Clip curves and turn lining to outside. Baste top of lining at waist to prevent slipping. Turn dress right side out. Press skirt hem lamé side down (lamé will stick to iron).

6. Carefully pull dress on over angel's head; hand-baste around neck, waist and each wrist, pulling threads to gather. Knot gathering threads.

7. "Pinch up" bottom of skirt at side seams on both sides, hand-basting about 2" of seam from bottom up. Pull threads tightly to gather and knot.

8. Right sides facing, sew satin shawl to lamé shawl, leaving open between notches. Clip corners; turn right side out. Press shawl from satin side; stitch opening closed.

Halo

1. Fold satin halo in half lengthwise, right sides facing. Stitch to form tube and turn right side out with loop puller or small safety pin.

2. Insert chenille stem; clip off excess with wire cutters.

3. Wrap beading wire around entire length of halo; clip off excess with wire cutters. Bring ends of halo together to form circle; secure with hot glue, holding ends together until glue cools and sets.

Finishing

1. Hot-glue braided trim around neck, waist and wrists, coating cut ends of trim with a small amount of glue to keep them from unraveling.

2. Hot-glue bows to sides of skirt at tops of "pinched" seams.

3. Drape shawl around shoulders (lamé side is "right" side), dropping drape low enough in back to leave room for wings. Secure shawl to body with dots of hot glue at shoulders, underarms and back, shaping and pleating with glue as needed.

4. Hot-glue wings to back just above drape and no higher than neckline of dress.

5. Apply a drop of hot glue to back of head and attach halo. Keep halo from resting on front of head (this will allow halo to appear to "float"). Apply a drop of glue to top of left hand; attach dove. Reinforce hot glue at halo and hand with craft glue to ensure good adhesion to porcelain. ✳

Pattern on pages 127-129

From the tip of her feathered wings to the hem of her corrugated paper dress, this sweet angel is dressed in pure white!

Snow-White Angel Ornament

Design by Kathy Wegner

Materials
- 6" x 5" white corrugated paper
- 4" x 3" translucent paper
- 1½" square of peach craft foam
- Rubber stamp
- White ink pad
- White embossing powder
- 1 sheet plain white typing paper
- 4 white feathers
- 2 (6") lengths Mini-Curl curly doll hair
- 2" strand white pearls
- Fiskars paper edgers with Scallop and Seagull edges
- Mounting Memories Keepsake Glue from Beacon Adhesives
- Hand-sewing needle and white floss or thread
- Thick tacky glue
- Candle or heat tool

Project Notes
Refer to photo throughout.

Use tacky glue unless instructed otherwise.

Instructions
1. Referring to patterns (page 130), cut one body from white corrugated paper, cutting bottom edge with scallop paper edgers and remainder of design with scissors; cut one apron from translucent paper, cutting bottom edge with seagull paper edgers and remainder of design with scissors; using scissors, cut one face from peach craft foam.

2. Stamp design in white ink onto apron. Place apron on a piece of typing paper and immediately sprinkle wet stamped design with embossing powder. Carefully pour excess powder back into jar.

3. Following manufacturer's instructions, carefully heat stamped design until it is melted and shiny; let cool.

4. Glue foam face to corrugated head. Glue two feathers to each wing. Glue curly hair around face. Glue pearl string above hair over top of head. Using Keepsake Glue, glue apron to corrugated body (tacky glue may make translucent paper wrinkle).

5. With needle and thread, sew hanging loop through top of angel; knot. ✳

Patterns on page 130

T

This sweet angel is accented with gold blanket stitch, gold buttons, a gold bow and gold halo, making her simply priceless!

Gold Felt Joy Angel

Design by Chris Malone

Materials

❤ Rainbow Felt Classic from Kunin Felt:
  1 sheet harvest gold #J55
  ½ sheet white #550
  ½ sheet apricot #394
❤ DMC 6-strand embroidery floss:
  Black #310
  Peach #353
  Medium golden olive #831
  Very dark terra cotta #3777
  Metallic gold #5282
❤ 2 (3mm) black beads
❤ Decorative gold metallic buttons: 2 (¾") and 1 (½")
❤ 5" metallic gold braided cord
❤ 10" (⅝"-wide) metallic gold wire-edge ribbon
❤ Polyester fiberfill
❤ Powdered cosmetic blusher
❤ Cotton-tip swab
❤ ¾" bone ring
❤ Embroidery needle
❤ Craft glue

Project Notes

Refer to photo throughout.

All stitching is done with 2 strands embroidery floss.

Instructions

1. Referring to patterns (page 131),
cut two heads and four legs from apricot felt, four wings and one of each letter from white felt, and two bodies from harvest gold.

2. Place letters on front of body; hold in place with pins or small dots of glue. Using metallic gold floss throughout, work blanket stitch around each letter and sew smaller gold button to center of O in "JOY."

3. Pin legs together in pairs. Using peach floss, sew together with blanket stitch; do not stuff.

4. Pin body pieces together wrong sides facing, with legs sandwiched between body halves at center bottom. Using medium golden olive floss, blanket stitch body halves together, catching tops of legs in stitches. Before closing body, stuff lightly with polyester fiberfill.

5. Pin wing pieces together in pairs; blanket stitch pieces together with metallic gold floss; do not stuff. Referring to dots on pattern, attach wings to body by positioning large gold button atop wing and sewing through all layers.

6. Using black floss, sew black beads to one apricot round for eyes; add mouth with French knot of very dark terra cotta floss. Blush cheeks lightly with cosmetic blusher applied with cotton-tip swab. Pin heads together, wrong sides facing; join with peach blanket stitch, stuffing lightly with polyester fiberfill before closing. Glue head to top of body, overlapping body ½".

7. For halo, overlap ends of gold braided cord ¼"; glue or sew together in ring. (If braid tends to ravel, coat cut ends with glue first and let dry.) Sew or glue halo to back of head.

8. Tie gold ribbon in bow; trim ends in a V and glue bow to neck

9. Sew bone ring to back of angel. Hang angel from wall, or slip ornament hanger in ring and use angel as a tree ornament. ✳

Patterns on page 131

Tack notes to your refrigerator with this colorful angel magnet dressed in a bouquet of flowers!

Flower Angel Magnet

Design by Judy Atwell

Materials

- 1¾" porcelain doll head
- 1" round button magnet
- 12" white chenille stem
- 2 (5½") squares polyester white Twinkle cloth
- 4 (1½"-diameter) silk flowers
- 2½" silk flower
- 3" piece narrow lace trim
- 3 (6") pieces coordinating satin picot-edge ribbon
- 4 (⅜") brass heart charms
- Small piece of florist's foam
- Wire cutters
- Hand-sewing needle and white thread
- Hot-glue gun

Project Note

Refer to photo throughout.

Instructions

1. Using wire cutters, cut flowers and leaves from stems. Set flowers aside.

2. Form florist's foam to fit inside doll's head and neckline, leaving about ½" protruding beyond neckline. Gently pull foam out; apply some glue and replace it in head.

3. Glue lace around neckline over shoulders and around back.

4. Cut chenille stem in half; twirl ends of each piece together and form each in a wing shape; twists should meet at center back.

5. Cover each form with Twinkle cloth, gathering fabric firmly at the twist. With needle and thread, sew gathers securely in place; wrap thread tightly around gathered fabric at twist and knot. Trim excess fabric from wings.

6. Glue wings to back of doll head. Glue magnet to back of wings. Glue one of the 1½" flowers into the foam on one side under the neckline; add a second on the other side in the same manner; glue a third to the front.

Where there are empty spaces, glue two petals together to fill them in.

7. Glue larger flower to bottom of doll. As needed, glue petals together to fill spaces.

8. Stack the ribbons on top of one another; apply glue at one end and glue ribbons up into the bottom flower, pressing some petals into the glue. Glue a tiny heart charm to each ribbon end.

9. Glue remaining flower upside down on top of doll's head for hat. Glue remaining heart charm at doll's neckline. ✤

Whether you set this little angel on your desk at work or on a shelf at home, she's sure to lighten your heart every time you set eyes on her!

Li'l Angel

Design by Helen L. Rafson

Materials

- 7" circle off-white lightweight fabric
- Matching thread and hand-sewing needle
- Polyester fiberfill
- Pantyhose
- 1½" Styrofoam ball
- Dried Spanish moss
- 7⅞" strand 2mm pearls
- 2 (5mm) black half-round cabochons
- Pink powdered cosmetic blusher
- Cotton-tip swab
- 2" round white Battenburg doily from Wimpole Street Creations
- 7½" piece (¼"-wide) metallic gold ribbon
- Seam sealant
- ½" white ribbon rose
- 2 pairs 2½" green silk leaves
- Aleene's fusible webbing
- Aleene's tacky glue
- Iron

Project Notes

Refer to photo throughout.

Let glue dry before proceeding with next step.

Instructions

1. Fold edges of fabric circle to wrong side ¼" all around. Sew running stitch around edges; do not cut or knot thread. Pull thread ends to gather circle, stuffing with polyester fiberfill. Pull thread to close stuffed circle tightly. Knot thread. Stitch opening closed.

2. Fit pantyhose tightly and smoothly over Styrofoam ball, gathering excess together. Twist excess several times. Tie and knot thread around excess stocking; cut excess stocking away. Using points of scissors, very carefully poke hole into ball through gathered stocking and tuck as much stocking as possible up into hole.

3. Glue Spanish moss hair to stocking-covered ball. Trim evenly.

4. Wrap pearl strand around head for halo; glue together in back.

5. Glue half-round black cabochon eyes to face. Apply blusher to cheeks with cotton-tip swab.

6. For collar, glue doily to stuffed circle over opening. Glue head atop doily collar.

7. Tie gold ribbon in a bow; trim ends at an angle and treat with seam sealant. Glue ribbon rose to center of bow. Glue bow with rose at center front of angel's neckline.

8. For wings, trace around two leaves onto fusible webbing; cut out webbing leaves slightly smaller all around. Fuse webbing leaves to wrong side of two silk leaves; peel off paper backing and fuse remaining leaves in place, wrong side of leaf facing webbing. Glue leaf wings to back of angel. ✳

T his little sweetie's pretty pink ruffles make her look like she's decked out in soft cotton candy! Craft her for a sweet touch of Victoriana!

Cotton Candy Angel

Design by Veleta Stafney

Materials
- Wooden doll pin and doll stand from Forster Inc.
- 1⅜" (⅜"-thick) wooden heart cutout
- 1¼" wooden ball knob
- Ceramcoat Gleams Paint from Delta Technical Coatings:
  Pearl finish #02 601
  Pinkie pearl finish #02 612
- Ceramcoat acrylic paints from Delta Technical Coatings:
  Adobe red #2046
  Medium flesh #2126
  White #2505
  Black #2506
- Ceramcoat satin-finish interior varnish
- ¼" paintbrushes
- 5½" (¾"-wide) pink-pearl-and-white lace ribbon
- 6" x 2½-yard strip shimmering pink tulle
- 2¾ yards (2"-wide) iridescent double-pleated lace
- Winter white Mini-Curl doll hair from One & Only Creations
- 3 (¾") pink iridescent silk flowers
- 1" pink silk flower
- 1" pink bow with pearl
- 4" strand pink 3mm pearls
- Black fine-point permanent marking pen
- Stylus
- Toothpick
- Hand-sewing needle and white thread
- Cotton-tip swabs
- Tacky glue
- Wire cutters

**Cotton Candy Angel
Facial Detail**

Project Notes
Refer to photo throughout.

Let all paints and ink dry between coats and applications.

Instructions
1. Glue doll stand on top of wooden heart; point of heart should be at center back. Glue doll pin into stand with split at center front. Paint doll pin with pearl finish and doll stand and heart with pinkie pearl.

2. Paint ball knob medium flesh. Referring to facial detail drawing dot on eyes using stylus dipped in black paint. Using cotton-tip swab to apply adobe red, lightly blush cheeks. Add nose and eyelashes with fine-point pen. Highlight eyes and cheeks with tiny dots of white paint applied with tip of toothpick.

3. Coat painted head, body and stand with varnish.

4. Cut pearl-and-lace ribbon in half. Glue half up front of doll pin, covering split; glue other half over back, covering split.

5. For dress, cut one piece pink tulle 1½ yards x 4". Fold in half lengthwise; sew basting stitch along fold and pull thread ends to gather

tulle tightly. Place around doll ⅜" below neck. Pull gathers tight and knot in center back.

6. For collar, cut 9" piece from double-pleated lace; set aside. Clip and remove threads down middle of remaining pleated lace. Sew basting stitch down one long edge; pull gathers and place around neck. Tighten gathers and knot at center back.

7. Cut several 3" strands of hair; twist in center and glue to top of head. Add hair to sides and back, filling in evenly. Trim as needed.

8. Cut 9" section from tulle and set aside for bow tie. For wings, tie remaining tulle in four-loop bow, tying center with small scrap strip of tulle. Trim tails to 2". Glue bow to back of neck.

9. Cut stems from flowers with wire cutters. Glue ¾" flowers over hair off to one side. Glue bow with pearl at neckline.

10. Sew basting stitch along center of remaining 9" piece of pleated lace; place around doll pin just above stand. Pull gathers tight and knot at center back. Glue pearls around gathered ribbon over basting stitch. Glue 1" flower at base of feet over center of pleated, gathered lace. ✳

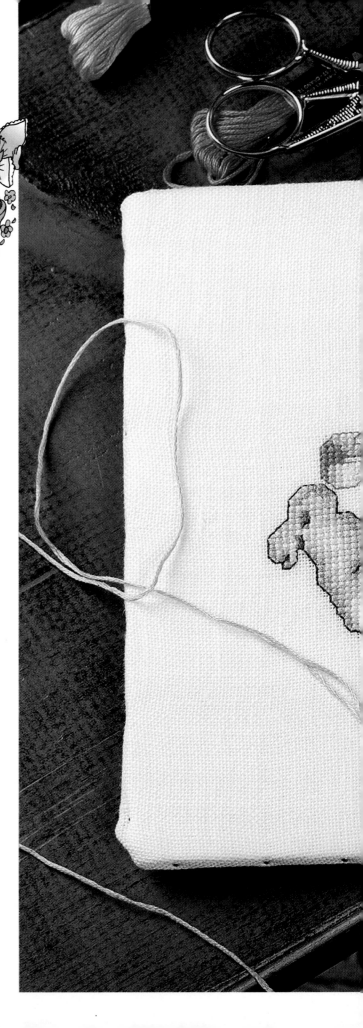

Cross-stitchers will treasure this beautiful piece depicting a cherub holding a bouquet of flowers.

Cherub With Flowers

Design by Ursula Michael

Materials

- ♥ 15" x 14" piece white 28-count linen from Zweigart
- ♥ DMC 6-strand embroidery floss as listed in color key
- ♥ #4 metallic braid from Kreinik Mfg. Co. Inc. as listed in color key
- ♥ Tapestry needle
- ♥ Mounting board, frame and mat as desired

Stitch Count

84 W x 73 H

Design Area

6" W x 5¼" H

Instructions

1. Fold fabric in quarters to find center; mark with pin or basting stitch. Match center of fabric to center of charted design (page 122) and begin stitching at this point.

2. Referring to charted design, complete all cross stitches using 2 strands floss, 1 strand braid, or a blended needle of 1 strand braid and 1 strand floss, and making each stitch over two fabric threads.

3. Using 1 strand floss throughout, add back-stitch, using very dark shell pink for flowers and hearts, medium Wedgewood for streamer and very dark beige brown for all other backstitch.

4. Block, mount and frame stitched design as desired. ✳

Chart on page 122

Cherub with Flowers
Continued from page 120

Continued from page 120

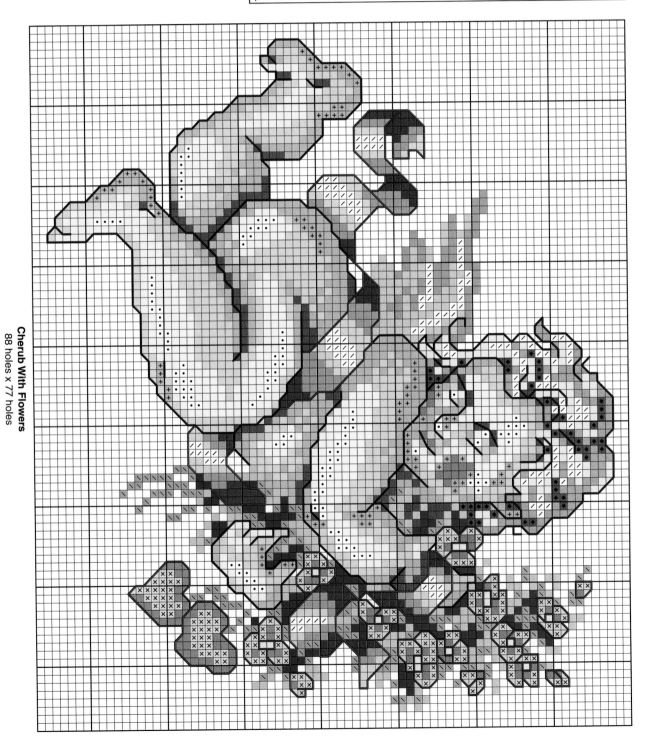

COLOR KEY

6-Strand Embroidery Floss

- ⊡ White #000
- ■ Very dark pistachio green #319
- ■ Light coral #352
- ✦ Dark hazelnut brown #420
- ▦ Sky blue #519
- ▢ Light topaz #726
- ▤ Medium old gold #729
- ▢ Light peach #754
- ▢ Very light pearl gray #762
- ▢ Ultra very light blue #828
- ▦ Light tawny #951
- ▨ Medium yellow green #3347
- ▨ Light yellow green #3348
- ■ Medium wedgewood #3760
- ▨ Very dark desert sand #3772
- ▤ Medium desert sand #3773
- ✚ Pink peach #3824
- ╱ Very dark shell pink #221 Backstitch
- ╱ Very dark beige brown #838 Backstitch
- ╱ Medium wedgewood #3760 Backstitch

#4 Metallic Braid

- ☑ Pearl #032

Blended Needle

- ☒ 1 strand star pink braid #092 plus
  1 strand light salmon #761 floss

Color numbers given are for DMC 6-strand embroidery floss and #4 metallic braid from Kreinik Manufacturing.

Cherub With Flowers
88 holes x 77 holes

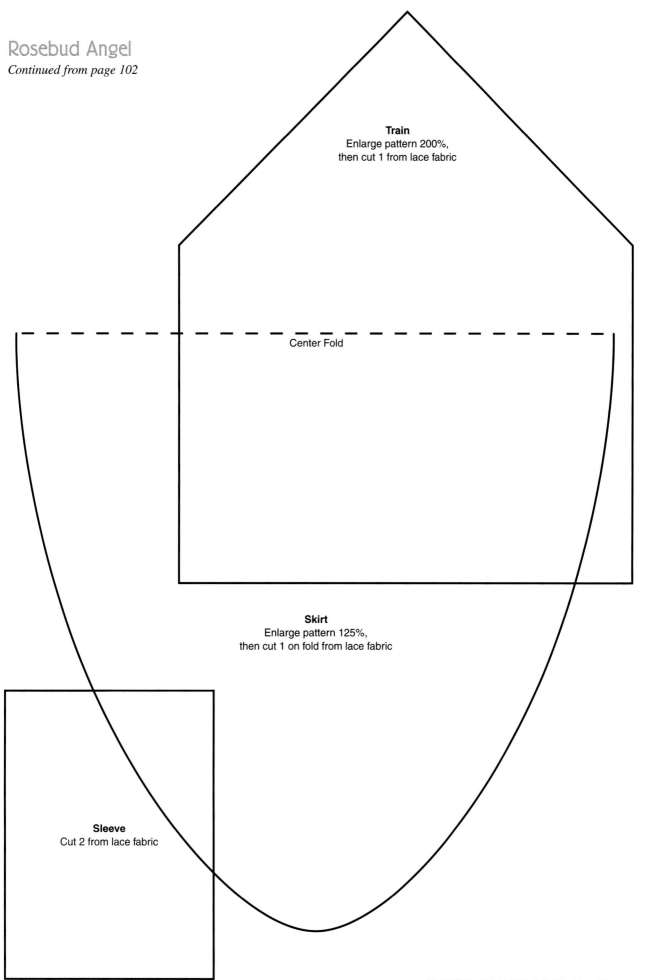

Train
Enlarge pattern 200%,
then cut 1 from lace fabric

Center Fold

Skirt
Enlarge pattern 125%,
then cut 1 on fold from lace fabric

Sleeve
Cut 2 from lace fabric

Victorian Lace Angel

My Guardian Angel Frame

Continued from page 109

My Guardian Angel Frame
Enlarge 125%

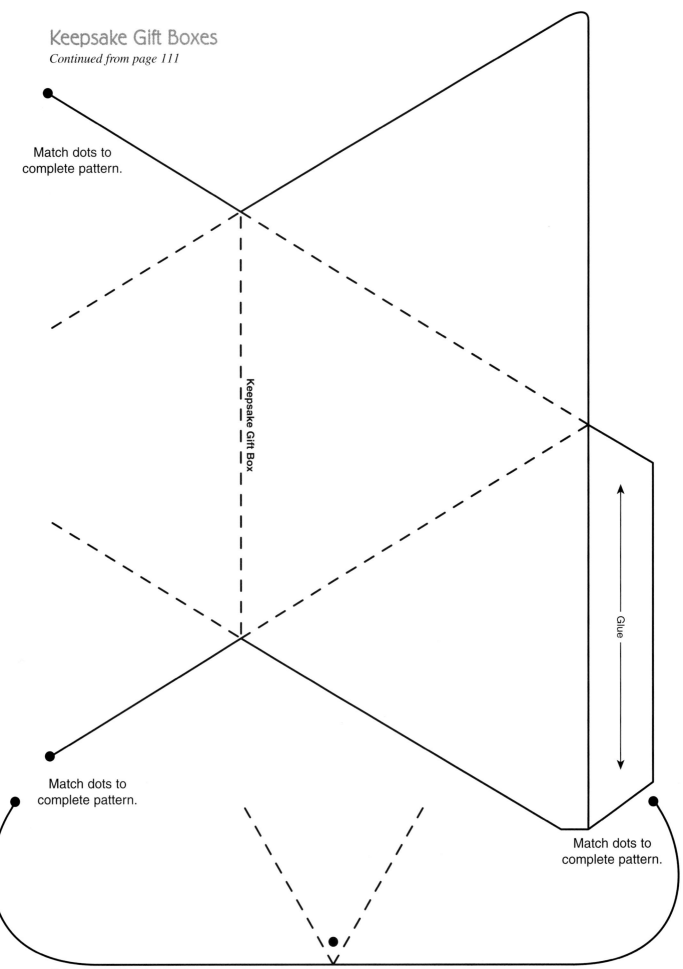

Match dots to
complete pattern.

Keepsake Gift Box

Glue

Match dots to
complete pattern.

Match dots to
complete pattern.

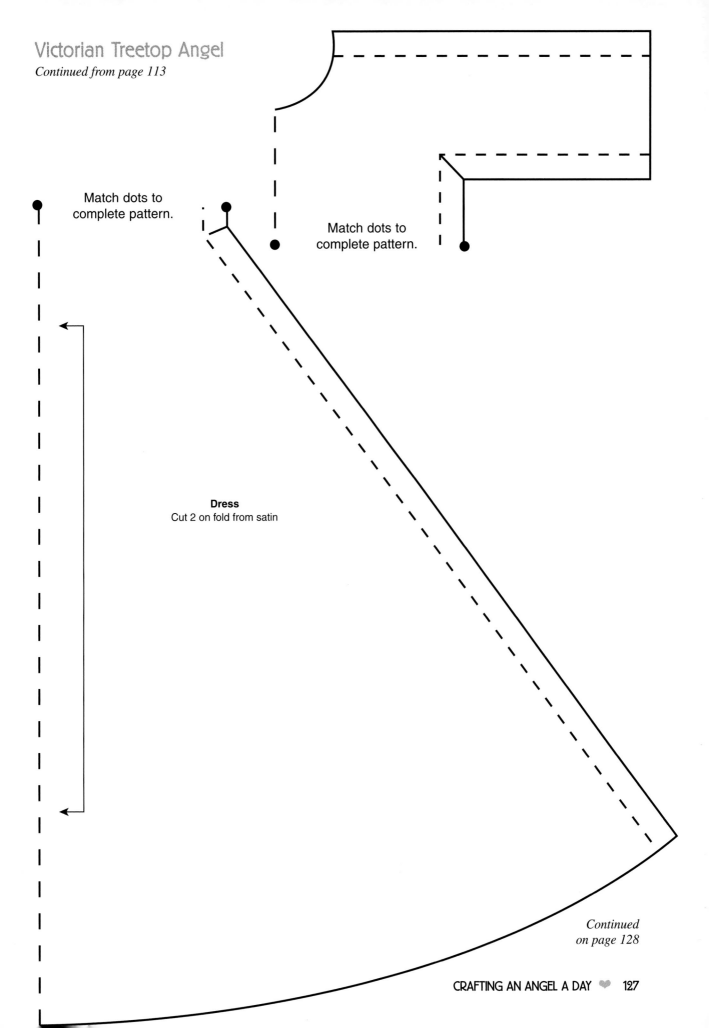

Victorian Treetop Angel

Continued from page 113

Match dots to
complete pattern.

Match dots to
complete pattern.

Dress
Cut 2 on fold from satin

*Continued
on page 128*

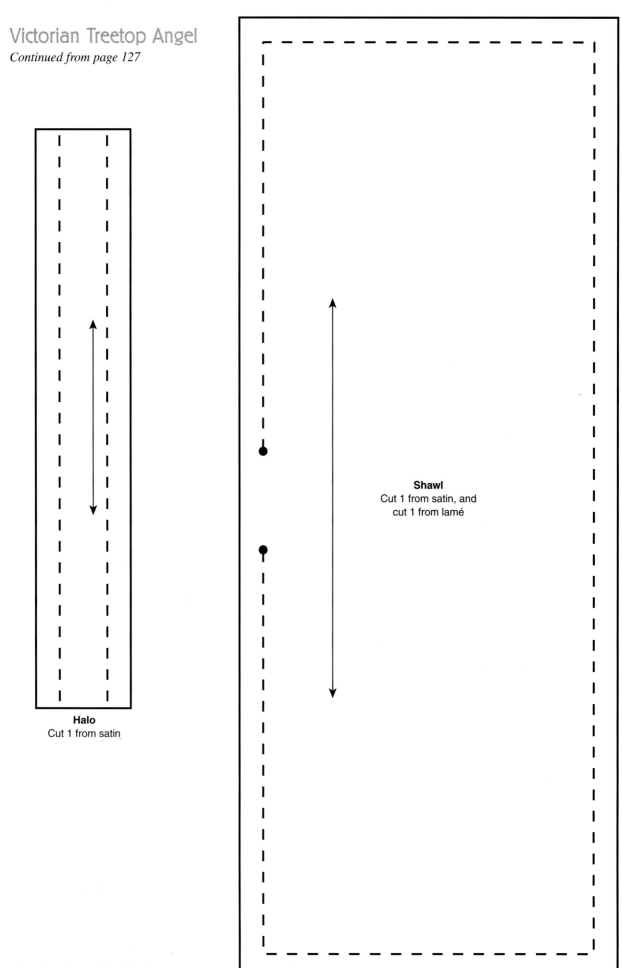

Victorian Treetop Angel
Continued from page 127

Halo
Cut 1 from satin

Shawl
Cut 1 from satin, and
cut 1 from lamé

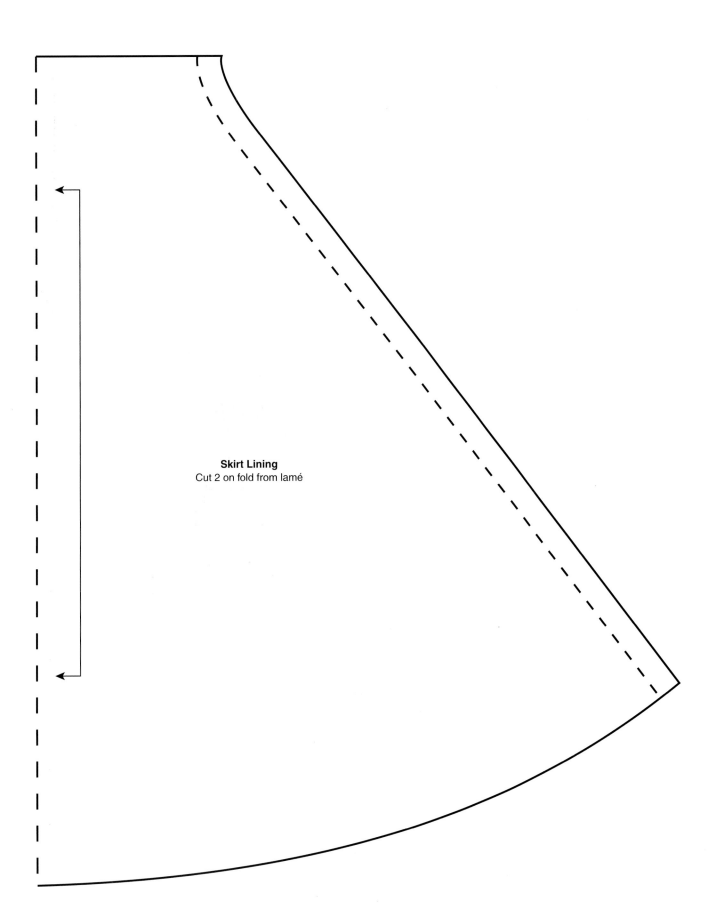

Skirt Lining
Cut 2 on fold from lamé

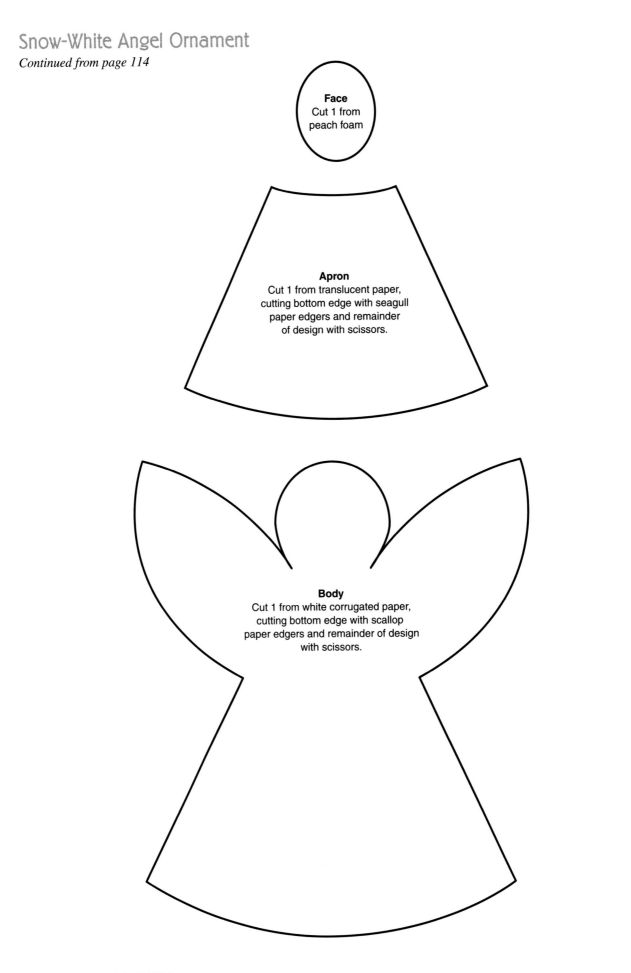

Face
Cut 1 from
peach foam

Apron
Cut 1 from translucent paper,
cutting bottom edge with seagull
paper edgers and remainder
of design with scissors.

Body
Cut 1 from white corrugated paper,
cutting bottom edge with scallop
paper edgers and remainder of design
with scissors.

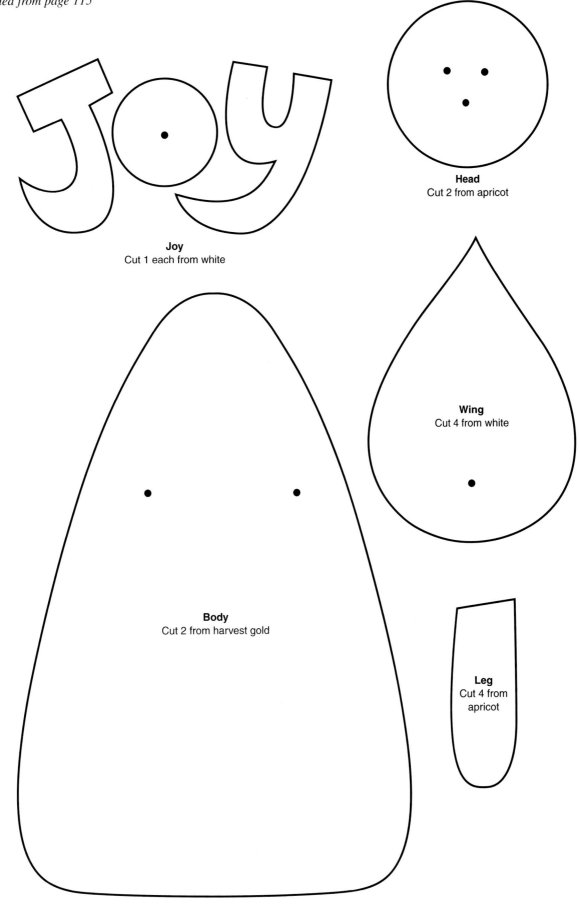

Joy
Cut 1 each from white

Head
Cut 2 from apricot

Wing
Cut 4 from white

Body
Cut 2 from harvest gold

Leg
Cut 4 from apricot

Angels are forever busy at work, helping all God's children! This collection of delightful angels celebrates just a few of the many occupations we crafters share.

Career ANGELS

Make this sign as a gift of appreciation for the "angel" who cares for your beloved pets.

The Doctor Is In!

Design by June Fiechter

Materials

- 💜 8" x 10" large oval slate #52 from Cape Cod Cooperage
- 💜 Graphite paper
- 💜 Ceramcoat acrylic paint by Delta Technical Coatings:
  Soft grey #02515
- 💜 Watercolor pencils from Staedtler:
  Maple #73
  Orange #4
  Light flesh #43
  Rose pink #25
  Gray #80

Turquoise #30
Dark brown #76
Black #9
Lime green #50
Royal blue #3
Scarlet #2
Gray-violet #8
Deep yellow #11
- 💜 Soft watercolor brush
- 💜 1" soft paintbrush
- 💜 Tissues
- 💜 Black permanent markers:
  Ultra-fine- and wide-point
- 💜 Matte clear acrylic spray finish

Project Note

Refer to photo throughout for placement.

Instructions

1. Using 1" soft paintbrush, basecoat front of slate with soft grey acrylic paint, *Note: Avoid totally covering edges.* Let dry.

2. Using graphite paper, transfer pattern onto painted slate.

3. Color picture with watercolor pencils as follows, using medium pressure and only applying color on the outer edges of each space: dog, doctor's hair and bone with maple; cat, doctor's halo and bird's beak with deep yellow; doctor's pants with royal blue; dog's nose and spots, doctor's shoes and center of stethoscope with black; cat's paws, center of cat's ear, highlight on cat's bottom and tail and portion under doctor's arm with orange; dog's collar with scarlet; bird with lime green; doctor's face and hands with light flesh; highlight on doctor's lab coat and shirt with gray; highlight on doctor's wings with turquoise; dog's leash and shading on dog's legs and ears with dark brown; and blush on doctor's cheeks and highlight on dog's muzzle with rose pink.

4. Add shading around doctor with gray-violet; shade around outside edge of plaque with maple.

5. With wet paintbrush, carefully go over each color, rinsing brush well between colors. While still wet, blot center of each color with a tissue to show highlight. Let dry thoroughly.

6. Draw around all outside edges with black ultra-fine-point permanent marker. Trace lines and draw dots for lettering with black wide-point permanent marker. Let dry.

7. Following manufacturer's instructions, spray with a light coat of clear matte acrylic spray. ✳

Angel Pot Holders

Designs by Helen L. Rafson

Spruce up your kitchen with this set of three charming pot holders!

Materials

Each Project
- Fusible webbing
- Pinking shears
- Black fine-point permanent marking pen
- Cotton-tip swab
- Pink powdered cosmetic blusher
- Seam sealant
- Tacky craft glue
- 2½" metallic gold cord
- Gold sewing thread
- Hand-sewing needle
- Sewing machine with zigzag stitch
- Iron
- Pliers

Sewing Angel
- 7" x 9" navy blue pot holder from Charles Craft Kitchen Products
- Fabric scraps: red print, light pink solid and blue-and-white check or plaid
- "A Stitch in Time" Dress It Up decorative buttons from Jesse James Co.
- Flat 2-hole buttons: 2 (⅜") navy blue 7 (½") yellow
- 6¾" piece (⅛"-wide) navy satin ribbon
- 14" piece (⅝"-wide) Captain's Stripe navy-and-gold ribbon from C.M. Offray and Son
- Matching sewing threads

Teaching Angel
- 8" square cream pot holder
- Fabric scraps: red print, green print and light pink solid
- "Pencil Box" Dress It Up decorative buttons from Jesse James Co.
- 6¾" piece (⅛"-wide) gold satin ribbon
- 7 (⁷⁄₁₆") red-brown flat 2-hole buttons
- A, B and C buttons from Cousin Corporation of America
- 6 (¾") gold 5-point star spangles from Nicole
- 14½" piece (⅝"-wide) Measure Up

measuring-tape ribbon from C.M. Offray and Son
- Metallic gold sewing thread or floss
- Matching sewing threads

Cooking Angel
- 7" x 9" hunter green pot holder from Charles Craft Kitchen Products
- Fabric scraps: red print, light pink solid, gold print and cream solid
- 1¾" piece (⅛"-wide) cream satin ribbon
- 2¾" piece (⅛"-wide) cream crochet edging or lace
- "In the Kitchen" Dress It Up decorative buttons from Jesse James Co.
- 6¾" piece (⅛"-wide) green satin ribbon
- 11½" piece (⅝"-wide) Status Strip green-and-red ribbon from C.M. Offray and Son
- 7 (⁷⁄₁₆") brown flat 2-hole buttons
- Matching sewing threads

Project Notes

Refer to photo throughout for placement.

"Gold thread" refers to gold-color cotton sewing thread; metallic gold thread will be referred to as such.

Sew on buttons and charms with matching thread unless instructed otherwise.

Sewing Angel

1. Referring to patterns (page 152), trace pieces onto wrong side of fusible webbing. Following manufacturer's instructions, fuse webbing to wrong sides of fabrics, fusing wings onto blue-and-white check, dress onto red print, and hands, feet and face onto pink solid. Cut out, cutting wings with pinking shears.

2. Using fine-point marking pen, outline wings and dress with dashed line to simulate stitching. Draw eyes, eyelashes and mouth on pink face. Blush cheeks by applying a little cosmetic blusher with a cotton-tip swab.

3. Fuse wings, then head, hands, feet and dress to pot holder.

4. Using sewing machine threaded

with gold thread throughout, zigzag around pot holder on edging. Reset machine to "tighten" zigzag; using same gold thread and referring to pattern, zigzag a "chain" from hand to hand across front of angel.

5. Sew decorative buttons to "chain," reinforcing with glue as needed to hold pieces securely, and snapping off shanks with pliers as needed so buttons and charms will lay flat.

6. Sew navy blue buttons to angel's

Continued on page 152

W

hen you plant your garden, leave room for angels to dance!

Gardening Angel

Design by Chris Malone

Materials

- ⅓ yard homespun plaid fabric
- 5" x 8" piece natural muslin
- 8½" piece (7"-wide) ecru lace
- Matching 3"-diameter round ecru lace doily
- Polyester fiberfill
- 1 cup plastic doll pellets
- Pink cosmetic blusher
- Cotton-tip swab
- 4 yards jute twine
- #5 or #6 metal knitting needle
- 8 (5") sprigs preserved eucalyptus
- Thin craft wire
- 3" grapevine wreath
- 24" piece cream (¹⁄₁₆"-wide) satin ribbon
- 1½" x 3" twig basket with handle
- 8 small silk flowers, some with leaves
- A few cream-colored dried flowers such as statice
- 2 (1¼") birds
- Scraps of dried Spanish moss
- 2 (4") rusty garden tools
- 1½" x 2¼" terra-cotta watering can
- Black fine-tip permanent marking pen
- Sewing machine (optional)
- Hand-sewing needle
- Matching sewing threads
- Oven
- Hot-glue gun
- Craft glue
- Masking tape

Project Note

Refer to photo throughout for placement.

Angel's Head & Body

1. Fold natural muslin in half. Referring to pattern (page 153), trace head onto doubled muslin. Pin fabric to hold layers securely. Sewing by hand or machine, stitch on traced lines, leaving bottom open. Cut out ⅛" from seam; clip curves and turn head right side out. Stuff firmly and stitch opening closed.

2. Using fine-point marking pen, dot on eyes; add eyelashes, eyebrows and "freckles." Apply blusher to cheeks with cotton-tip swab.

3. From plaid fabric, cut four sleeves and two 6½" x 9½" rectangles for dress.

4. Pin dress rectangles together, right sides facing. Sew together along both long edges and one short edge, leaving ¼" seam allowance.

5. So that angel will stand, box bottom of dress, referring to Fig. 1 (page 153): Match bottom of seam with adjacent side seam; flatten to form a point. Pin seams together and sew 1" from point, perpendicular to seams, through both layers. Repeat on other side. Trim seam

allowances to ¼"; turn dress right side out.

6. Press under ½" hem at neck (open) edge. Pour pellets into bottom of dress; stuff remainder of dress with polyester fiberfill, stuffing firmly next to pellets and lightly toward top.

7. Hand-sew gathering stitches around neck edge. Insert head into neck opening and pull thread ends to gather dress snugly around neck. Knot securely. Tack dress to neck in a few spots.

Hair, Apron & Sleeves

1. For hair, wrap jute evenly around knitting needle; secure ends with a small place of tape. Wet jute lightly and heat in a 300-degree oven for 25 minutes. Remove and leave jute on needle until cool; gently slip curls off needle. Apply craft glue to top and back of head; gently loop curls over and around head, pressing to set in place.

2. For apron, hand-sew a line of gathering stitches 1" down from top of lace. Pull thread until apron measures 2" wide and knot thread. Apply glue to back of gathering stitches and press to front neck of dress. Fold center top of apron down at stitch line and glue one silk flower with leaves at top of fold.

3. For each sleeve, pin two pieces together right sides facing; sew together using ¼" seam allowance and leaving straight edge open. Clip curves; turn sleeves right side out.

4. Press under ¾" hem at bottom of each sleeve. Lightly stuff top of sleeve. Hand-sew line of gathering stitches ½" from fold; pull tightly to gather sleeves closed and knot thread. Hot-glue top of each sleeve to front of shoulders.

Finishing & Assembly

1. For wings, strip bottom two leaves from each eucalyptus branch. Hold four branches together; wrap

Continued on page 153

Bedtime Angel

Design by Veleta Stafney

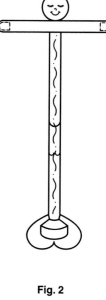

Fig. 1

Fig. 2

Materials

- Woodsies wooden products from Forster Inc.:
  3 jumbo craft sticks
  Large (11/4") circle
  Doll stand
  Large (2" x 1") rectangle
  Craft stick
- 23/4"-wide x 1/4"-thick wooden heart with "ruffled"edge
- 1 pair 6" wooden wings
- Ceramcoat acrylic paints from Delta Technical Coatings:
  Indiana rose #2018
  Adobe red #2046
  Lisa pink #2084
  White #2505
  Black #2506
- 1/2" paintbrush
- Stylus or wooden toothpick
- Pink sewing thread and hand sewing needle
- Ceramcoat satin-finish acrylic varnish from Delta Technical Coatings
- 5 yard x 6" strip pink tulle
- 4" white heart-shaped doily from Wimpole Street Creations
- White mini curl doll hair
- 7 (3/8") pink ribbon rosettes with green ribbon leaves
- Sparkle glaze from Delta Technical Coatings
- Extra-fine-point black permanent marking pen
- Small piece of sea sponge
- Tacky craft glue
- Cotton swab
- Paper towels

Pattern Notes

Refer to photo throughout for placement.

Let paint, ink and varnish dry between coats and applications.

Angel Body

1. *Body:* Overlap two jumbo craft sticks by 1"; glue together. Trim off one end in a straight line (this will be bottom edge of body). Glue top half of circle to top of rounded end of body for head.

2. Paint assembled body and head with Indiana rose. Using black marking pen, draw curvy lines down center of body to define legs, referring to Fig. 1.

3. Glue doll stand to center of "ruffled" heart; paint black. Referring to Fig. 2, use stylus and Lisa pink paint to draw border of comma strokes, dots and hearts around outer edge of heart.

4. Fill opening in doll stand with glue to depth of 3/4". Gently push bottom (flat) edge of body into glue; hold in place until it is secure.

5. Draw eyes, eyelashes, nose and mouth on face with extra-fine-line marking pen. Dip brush into adobe red; paint on paper towel until almost no paint remains in brush. Blush cheeks with nearly dry brush. Using stylus or toothpick, add tiny

white highlight dot to each cheek.

6. *Arms:* Lightly pencil off hands 1" from each end of remaining jumbo craft stick; paint hands with Indiana rose and arms with white. Draw border of dashes and dots around hands with marking pen; glue center of arms to back of neck.

7. Varnish head, body, stand and arms.

Clothing & Wings

1. Cut 2-yard piece from one end of tulle. Sew a running stitch along one long edge; pull thread to gather tulle tightly. Place dress around body 5/8" below arms with opening in center back. Secure with knot and glue to hold.

Fig. 3

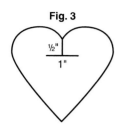

½"
1"

2. For second layer of dress, cut another 2-yard piece of tulle. Sew running stitch along one long edge and pull gathers tight. Place right below arms with opening in center back. Secure with knot and glue to hold.

3. For collar, referring to Fig. 3, cut ½" slit in heart doily; cut ½" slit in both sides. Glue doily collar around neck with slit in back.

4. Wrap three strands of hair around four fingers 15 times. Slide off fingers; twist in center. Tie in center with another 3" strand of hair and glue center of hair to top of head. Repeat to fill in back of head and spot glue hair around face. Trim any loose ends.

5. Paint wooden wings white. Dip sponge into Lisa pink; lightly sponge over wings. Draw border of S-shaped lines and dots around edges. Varnish wings. Glue wings to back of arms.

Finishing

1. *Sign:* Glue rectangle to top of craft stick. Paint white. With black marking pen, write "Guardian of Your Dreams" on sign. Paint dots of Lisa pink around edge of sign and down craft stick. Varnish sign; glue to one hand.

2. From remaining tulle, tie two bows, leaving one with 4" tails. Glue this to front of collar at waist. Trim tails of other bow; glue to top of stand.

3. Glue three ribbon rosettes to hair; glue one to sign, one to other hand and one to center of each bow.

4. Using cotton-tip swab, apply sparkle glaze highlights to dress, hair, bows and roses. ✱

Express your appreciation for your child's teacher with this special ornament!

Teacher's Treasure

Design by Chris Malone

Materials
- 4¼" x 3¼" framed wooden blackboard
- 1" wooden plug
- 1½"-wide wooden primitive star cutout
- Americana acrylic paints from DecoArt:
  White wash #DA2
  Antique gold #DA9
  Country blue #DA41
  Lamp black #DA67
  Base flesh #DA136
  Shading flesh #DA137
- Satin-finish varnish
- Paintbrushes:
  ½" flat
  #0 liner
  Small stencil brush
- White graphite paper
- Fine-point black permanent marking pen
- Strawberry blonde Mini Curl doll hair from One & Only Creations
- 5" piece (24-gauge) gold wire
- 8" piece (⅜"-wide) white wire-edge ribbon
- 10" (³⁄₁₆"-thick) decorative white twisted cording
- 2 small screw eyes
- Tape
- Craft glue or hot-glue gun

Project Note
Let all paints and finishes dry between paints and applications.

Painting
1. Using flat brush, base-coat blackboard frame with country blue, plug with base flesh (for face) and star with antique gold.

2. Following manufacturer's instructions and referring to pattern, transfer "My teacher is a blessing" onto blackboard with white graphite paper.

3. Thin a little white wash paint with water until it is the consistency of ink; using liner brush, paint letters with thinned paint. For dots on tips of letters, dip tip of paintbrush handle into undiluted white wash paint; dot paint onto letter. Use same method to add dots to blackboard frame.

4. Dip stencil into shading flesh; remove most of paint onto paper towel, then use brush to add cheeks to wooden face. Dot on two black dots for eyes and two white dots for cheek highlights.

5. Using fine-point marking pen, outline star with "squiggly" lines.

6. Coat painted pieces with varnish.

Assembly & Finishing
1. Insert screw eyes into top edge of frame 1" from ends.

2. Rub doll hair between fingers to frizz it. Apply glue to top of angel's head and press curls into glue.

3. Twist wire into a 1¼"-diameter circle for halo, twisting ends together. Glue twisted ends to back of head so halo extends above head.

4. Tie ribbon into a small bow; notch ribbon ends. Glue bow at bottom of face.

5. Glue face to lower left corner of frame and star to upper right corner.

6. Wrap tape around each end of cord; push each end through screw eye, back to front. Knot each end in front of screw eye; trim excess cord close to knot. ✳

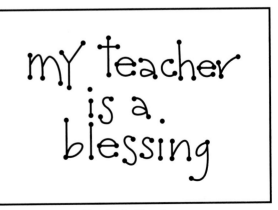

Teacher's Blessing

T iny seedlings need tender loving care. Give them a colorful home of their own with this windowsill box!

Windowsill Garden Angel

Design by June Fiechter

Continued on page 154

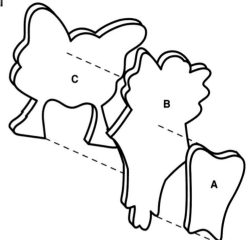

Fig. 1
Hot-glue angel pieces
together as shown

Materials
- Wooden CD crate
- 2 wooden handles from Ameroc
- 8 craft sticks cut in half
- 3 (1"-wide x ⁄₁₆"-thick) wooden stars from Walnut Hollow
- 12" x 4" piece (⁄₁₆"-thick) balsa wood
- 24-gauge wire:
  2½"
  2 (16")
- Stencil Magic Mini Dot Alphabet stencil #810 from Delta Technical Coatings
- Ceramcoat all-purpose sealer from Delta Technical Coatings
- Ceramcoat acrylic paints from Delta Technical Coatings:
  Fleshtone #2019
  Ivory #2036
- Sunbright yellow #2064
- Terra cotta #2071
- Territorial beige #2425
- Black #2506
- Purple dusk #2522
- Pink parfait #2525
- Light foliage green #2537
- Paintbrushes, including liner brush
- Matte-finish interior spray varnish from Delta Technical Coatings
- 3 (4⅛"-diameter) terra-cotta flowerpots
- Drill and drill bit to fit handle screws
- Hot-glue gun
- Screwdriver
- Fine #400 sandpaper
- Tack cloth
- Small razor-edge knife

Project Notes
Refer to photo throughout for placement.

Let all paints and finishes dry between coats and applications of adjacent colors unless instructed otherwise.

Wood Preparation
1. Referring to patterns (page 154), trace angel patterns onto balsa wood; cut out using razor-edge knife.

2. Sand balsa pieces, handles and crate surfaces that will be painted; wipe off dust with tack cloth. Apply one coat sealer to sanded wood

Continued on page 154

T

These sweet angels can easily be adapted to celebrate any occupation, or craft them as shown to honor teachers, beauticians and nurses!

Earth Angels

Designs by Bonnie Stephens

Materials
- ♥ Ceramcoat acrylic paints from Delta Technical Coatings:
  Forest green #2010
  Brown iron oxide #2023
  Tomato spice #2098
  Medium flesh #2126
  Butter cream #2523
  Village green #2447
  White #2505
  Black #2506
- ♥ Paintbrushes:
  ¾" flat
  10/0 liner
  Spatter brush
  #10 flat
- ♥ Fine-point black permanent marking pen
- ♥ Miracle sponge
- ♥ 2¼"-diameter wooden circle from Lara's Crafts
- ♥ 5" x 6" picture frame with 2" x 3" opening
- ♥ White 140-lb. watercolor paper
- ♥ Fabric scraps in country-style checks
- ♥ 18-gauge craft wire
- ♥ Craft drill with small bit
- ♥ Wire cutters
- ♥ Tacky craft glue
- ♥ Hot-glue gun

Project Notes
Refer to photo throughout for placement.

Use ¾" flat brush unless instructed otherwise.

For "thinned" paint, mix a small amount of desired color with enough water to create a mixture with the consistency of ink.

Let all paints and ink dry between applications.

"An Angel of a Beautician"
1. Paint frame village green. Paint circle medium flesh.

2. Referring to patterns (page 155), cut one pair wings from watercolor paper; cut also one 3" square. Paint all pieces with two or three coats of butter cream paint to give paper stability. With craft glue, glue painted paper square in frame opening.

3. Load #10 flat brush for shading: Dip corner of brush into brown iron oxide; blend on palette until paint is dark on one side of brush and blended out to no paint on other side. Using this brush, shade edges of wings and edge of paper inside frame opening.

4. Referring to patterns, cut one small tree and one large tree from miracle sponge. Dip in water to expand; squeeze out excess water. Paint one surface of each sponge with forest green and a little village green on tree and brown iron oxide on trunk. Press one painted sponge onto each side of frame.

5. Spatter frame lightly with thinned forest green paint keeping spatters off paper in center as much as possible.

6. Dot eyes on medium flesh head with wooden end of liner brush dipped in black. Redip between eyes to make eyes of uniform size.

7. For cheeks, dip stencil brush in tomato spice; scrub on paper towel until very dry. Scrub brush in circular motion on face to create cheeks. Add mouth with 10/0 liner and thinned tomato spice paint.

8. Dot berries onto trees with paintbrush handle dipped in tomato spice paint; add cluster of three smaller berries to collar. Using 10/0 liner brush, paint forest green comma-stroke leaves around berries on collar.

9. Using marking pen, add "stitching line" around edges of wings; write "An Angel of a Beautician" in frame opening.

10. Using craft glue, glue wings to frame front; hot-glue head over wings. Hot-glue Spanish moss hair to angel's head. Knot small pieces of fabric. Trim ends at an angle; hot-glue one to center front of chin and others to hair. Tie 3" bow from contrasting fabric; trim ends at an angle and hot-glue at center top of head.

11. Drill holes for hanger through top corners of wings and frame. Cut 12" piece of wire; bend into hanger and thread ends through holes in frame from back to front. Coil wire ends around paintbrush handle; slide coils off handle.

"An Angel of a Teacher"
1. Repeat steps 1–4 for Beautician Frame, painting frame black.

2. Repeat steps 6–9 for Beautician Frame, writing "An Angel of a Teacher" in frame opening. Make spectacles by wrapping two circles of wire next to each other so they fit over eyes; wrap wire ends of glasses around to back of head and hot-glue to secure.

3. Using craft glue, glue wings to frame front; hot-glue head over wings. Hot-glue Spanish moss hair to angel's head. Knot two small pieces of fabric. Trim ends at an angle; hot-glue one to center front of chin and one to hair.

4. Repeat step 11 for Beautician Frame.

"An Angel of a Nurse"
1. Repeat step 1 for Beautician Frame, painting frame tomato red.

Continued on page 155

Fun and versatile, these adorable gingerbread angels make great gifts for everyone who serves your family throughout the year!

Gingerbread Career Angels

Designs by Annie Lang

Materials
Tote Bag
- 13" x 13½" white canvas tote bag from BagWorks
- T-shirt painting board or cardboard covered with plastic to fit inside tote bag
- Fabric transfer pen or pencil
- Daler-Rowney/Robert Simmons Fabric Master paintbrushes:
  #2 flat scrubber #431F
  #2, #4 and #6 pointed round #431PR
  #1 liner #431L
- So-Soft acrylic fabric paints from DecoArt:
  White #DSS1
  Cadmium yellow #DSS3
  Cadmium orange #DSS4
  Calico red #DSS5
  Baby blue #DSS16
  Terra cotta #DSS22
  Black #DSS24
  Ultra deep blue #DSS27
  Grey sky #DSS28
- Fine-point black permanent textile marker (optional)

- Purchased or homemade 1½" wide heart-shaped sponge stamp
- Disposable plastic foam plate or paint palette

Flock of Angels
- 8" square 140-lb. watercolor paper
- Transfer pencil
- Assorted acid-free watercolor markers in same colors as fabric paints for tote bag
- Black fine-point marking pen
- Laminating plastic
- Double-sided adhesive sheet
- Magnetic sheeting
- Key chain
- 1½" pin back
- Wire ornament hanger hook
- 4" satin craft cord
- Miniature clothespin
- 4" x 8" colored construction paper
- ¼" round paper punch
- Decorative paper edgers
- Craft glue and/or cement

Color Choices

Nurse: Uniform, cap and thermometer are white. Paint stripes on sleeves and skirt with calico red; add white highlight to heart in her hand.

Business Guy: Suit and hat are grey sky; shirt collar and cuffs are baby blue; tie and hatband are ultra deep blue; briefcase is black with cadmium yellow trim; paper in his hand is white with black wavy lines.

Teacher: Blouse, chalk and heart on slate are white; hair and neck bows are calico red; skirt is baby blue. Slate has terra cotta frame and black slate.

Industrial Worker: Hard hat is cadmium yellow; T-shirt is white with calico red stripes on sleeves; coveralls are ultra deep blue; bucket and hammer head are grey sky; hammer handle is terra cotta; goggles are white with black frames (paint white over terra cotta face; redraw eyes and smile "behind" goggles).

Firefighter: Hat and coat are cadmium yellow; hose is cadmium orange and nozzle is grey sky.

Policewoman: Blouse is baby blue; skirt, tie and crown of hat are ultra deep blue; bill of hat and flashlight are black; megaphone is grey sky; arm patch, items in pocket and "glow" from flashlight are cadmium yellow; with #1 liner brush, add highlight lines to flashlight and bill of hat with white.

Surgeon: Scrubs are baby blue; clipboard is cadmium yellow; "charts" and mask are white; stethoscope is grey sky.

Businesswoman: Suit is ultra deep blue; shirt, cuffs and paper are white; pencil is cadmium yellow with black tip; briefcase is calico red.

Tote Bag

1. Referring to patterns (page 156) and following manufacturer's instructions, transfer complete design to front of tote bag, using fabric transfer pen or pencil.

2. Insert plastic-covered cardboard or T-shirt painting board into tote bag so surface of bag lays flat and smooth; secure with masking tape, rubber bands or pins as needed.

3. *All gingerbread characters:* Paint face, arms and legs with terra cotta. Using calico red and #4 round brush, add tiny cheeks (cheeks are even with eyes). Using black and #1 liner, add eyes and smile. Using #1 liner and white, add tiny highlight dots to cheeks. All hearts are calico red unless otherwise indicated; fill in all wings with white.

Continued on page 157

Where Angels Go...
People Follow!

Decorate cookies

Here's a great gift for someone who helps others pursue their dreams and make them come true!

Catch a Falling Star Sweatshirt

Design by Beth Wheeler

Materials
- White sweatshirt in desired size
- Fabric scraps:
  2 blue prints, desired flesh-tone, navy and yellow
- Fusible webbing
- Fusible tear-away stabilizer
- Machine-sewing threads:
  Navy blue rayon
  Flesh-tone rayon
  Black rayon
  Blue tweed rayon
  White all-purpose
  Monofilament
  Metallic silver
  Metallic gold
- Metallic 6-strand embroidery floss: gold and silver
- 3 small black buttons
- Air-soluble fabric marker or tailor's chalk
- Hand-sewing needle
- Sewing machine with zigzag stitch
- Iron

Project Note
Refer to photo throughout for placement.

Appliqués
1. Referring to patterns (at right and page 158), trace pieces onto wrong side of fusible webbing. Following manufacturer's instructions, fuse webbing to wrong sides of fabrics, fusing sleeve and dress to blue print A; cuff and hem to blue print B; face and hand to flesh-tone; shoe to navy; and star and hair to yellow print. Cut pieces out.

2. Position fabric cutouts on front of sweatshirt; fuse in place.

3. Position fabric stabilizer on wrong side of sweatshirt over pieced design; baste in place.

4. Thread sewing machine needle with silver metallic thread and bobbin with white all-purpose thread; satin stitch around star, omitting bottom left point held in hand.

5. Repeat step 4 to satin stitch around other pieces, using flesh-tone rayon for front edge of face and hand (except edge adjacent to sleeve), navy rayon for foot (except edge adjacent to hem) and blue tweed rayon for sleeve (including line between cuff and sleeve) and entire gown (including line between dress and hem).

6. Threading top of machine with gold metallic thread, satin stitch around hair, stitching next to the blue tweed stitching between gown and hair.

7. Carefully trim away excess fabric stabilizer from wrong side of sweatshirt.

Embroidery
1. Using fabric marking pen, mark angel's flight pattern, halo, yellow star's rays and positions of silver stars on front of sweatshirt.

2. Using 4 strands metallic embroidery floss throughout, hand-stitch

Falling Star
Cut 1 from
yellow print

flight pattern and halo with gold running stitch and yellow star's rays with silver running stitch.

3. Using 3 strands metallic silver embroidery floss, straight stitch stars as desired.

4. Using black rayon thread throughout, satin stitch vertical mouth on star, stitching over mouth several times, and sewing black ball button to top of mouth. Sew remaining ball buttons in place for star's eyes.

5. Stitch angel's eye with satin stitch or large French knot.

Stripes
1. Piece together scraps from both blue prints to make two strips 2½" wide and long enough to fit around sleeves at sleeve-shoulder seam.

2. Press under ½" along both sides of both pieced strips.

3. Pin strips in place around sleeves, beginning and ending ½" from underarm seam.

4. Set sewing machine for a narrow zigzag stitch and thread machine with monofilament thread in needle and white thread in bobbin. Machine-stitch strips in place along both edges. ✳

Patterns on page 158

f you are the proud parent or grandparent of a ball-playing child, then you'll want to make and share this set of five all-star ornaments.

Sport Angel Ornaments

Designs by Sandra Graham Smith

Materials
- ♥ Brown paper grocery bag
- ♥ Polyester fiberfill
- ♥ Pinking shears
- ♥ Wire cutters
- ♥ Transfer paper
- ♥ Enamel craft paints: red, white, blue, black, green, orange, yellow, light pink and pink
- ♥ Gold glitter paint
- ♥ Paintbrush
- ♥ Fine-point permanent marking pens: black, white and red
- ♥ Small hole punch
- ♥ Tacky craft glue
- ♥ Several clip clothespins or small binder clips
- ♥ Gold star garland

Project Note
Let paints dry completely before adding final details with paints and markers.

Painting
1. Referring to patterns (pages 151, 158 and 159), use pinking shears to cut shapes for desired ornament from doubled layer of heavy brown paper. Set one aside for backing.

2. Following manufacturer's instructions, transfer desired pattern to front piece of heavy paper.

Referring to pattern and photo, paint design with acrylic paints as shown, painting all wings white and all faces and hands light pink.

3. Using gold glitter paint, paint halos.

4. Paint pink cheeks on each angel.

5. Using red marker, draw mouths on all ornaments; add stitches and seam lines to baseball.

6. Using white marker, add stitches and seam line to football.

7. Using black marker, add all other details—eyes, freckles, noses, and outlines. Also draw "stitching line" around ornament just inside pinked edges.

Assembly & Finishing
1. Leaving opening at bottom for stuffing, apply a fine line of glue around edges and glue matching cutouts together.

2. Lightly stuff ornaments with small pieces of fiberfill, using paintbrush handle to poke stuffing into ornament.

3. Glue opening closed; secure edges with clothespins or binder clips until glue is set.

4. Referring to patterns, punch holes for hanger where indicated. Thread star garland through holes for hanger. ✳

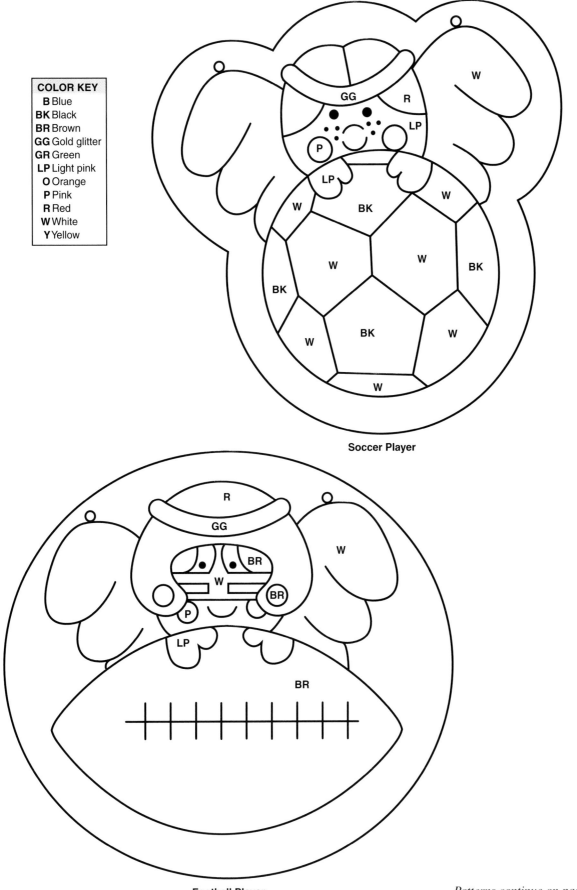

COLOR KEY
B Blue
BK Black
BR Brown
GG Gold glitter
GR Green
LP Light pink
O Orange
P Pink
R Red
W White
Y Yellow

Soccer Player

Football Player

Patterns continue on page 158

Angel Pot Holders
Continued from page 136

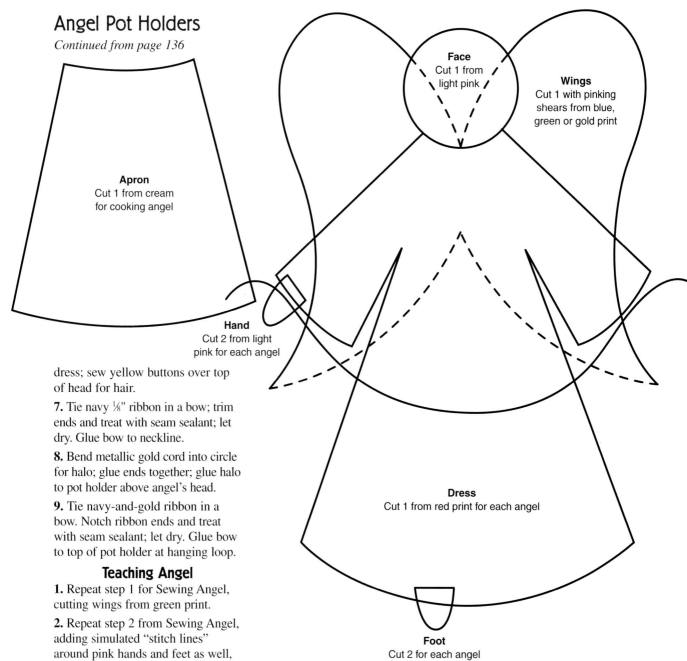

Apron
Cut 1 from cream
for cooking angel

Face
Cut 1 from
light pink

Wings
Cut 1 with pinking
shears from blue,
green or gold print

Hand
Cut 2 from light
pink for each angel

Dress
Cut 1 from red print for each angel

Foot
Cut 2 for each angel
from light pink

dress; sew yellow buttons over top of head for hair.

7. Tie navy ⅛" ribbon in a bow; trim ends and treat with seam sealant; let dry. Glue bow to neckline.

8. Bend metallic gold cord into circle for halo; glue ends together; glue halo to pot holder above angel's head.

9. Tie navy-and-gold ribbon in a bow. Notch ribbon ends and treat with seam sealant; let dry. Glue bow to top of pot holder at hanging loop.

Teaching Angel

1. Repeat step 1 for Sewing Angel, cutting wings from green print.

2. Repeat step 2 from Sewing Angel, adding simulated "stitch lines" around pink hands and feet as well, and fusing angel to pot holder on the diagonal with hanging loop at top.

3. Repeat step 3 from Sewing Angel.

4. Repeat steps 4–8 for Sewing Angel, making following changes:

• Use red thread for zigzag stitch around pot holder edging (not chain);

• Use ABC beads for buttons down front of dress;

• Use red-brown buttons for hair;

• Use gold ⅛" ribbon for neckline bow.

5. Tie measuring-tape ribbon in a bow; glue to top corner of pot holder.

6. Using metallic gold thread, sew star spangles to pot holder.

Cooking Angel

1. Repeat step 1 for Sewing Angel, cutting wings from gold print. Cut also one apron from cream fabric.

2. Repeat steps 2 and 3 from Sewing Angel, fusing cream apron atop dress.

3. Cut cream ribbon to fit across waist for "apron ties" and cut crochet edging to fit across bottom of apron. Treat ends with seam sealant; let dry. Glue ribbon and edging in place.

4. Repeat steps 4–8 for Sewing Angel, making following changes:

• Use red thread for zigzag stitch around pot holder edging (not chain);

• Omit buttons on dress;

• Use brown buttons for hair;

• Use green 1/8" ribbon for neckline bow.

5. Tie red-and-green striped ribbon in a bow. Notch ribbon ends and treat with seam sealant; let dry. Glue bow to top of pot holder at hanging loop. ✳

Gardening Angel
Continued from page 139

wire around bottom to secure. Repeat with remaining branches. Place wrapped ends together, end overlapping end, and wrap wire around both bunches. Glue wrapped center to back of angel; glue a few single leaves over wire to conceal it.

2. If grapevine wreath is too thick, cut it apart and re-form to make a 3"-diameter wreath with just three or four strands. Wrap ribbon around wreath; tie ends in a bow and let streamers hang down. Glue wreath to back of head for halo with ribbon streamers in back.

3. Glue a wisp of Spanish moss to top of wreath halo for nest; glue one bird to nest.

4. Glue center of doily in bottom of basket so edges of doily extend over sides of basket. Glue Spanish moss inside doily. Glue stem of silk flower into moss; repeat with additional silk and dried flowers until basket is full. Glue second bird over flowers. Glue or sew basket handle inside cuff of one sleeve so basket hangs down with bird in front.

5. Glue or tack tools to side of body under remaining arm as shown; glue or sew top of watering can to inside of cuff; glue sleeve over tool handles. ✲

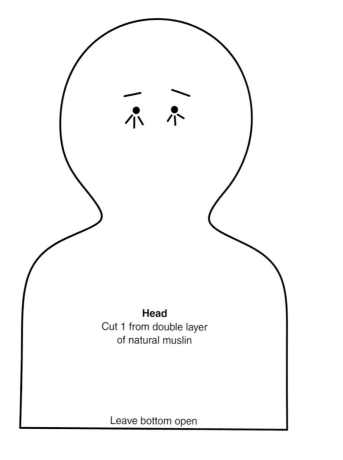

Head
Cut 1 from double layer
of natural muslin

Leave bottom open

Fig. 1

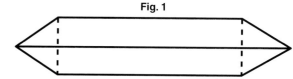

Sleeve
Cut 4 from plaid fabric

Windowsill Garden Angel

Continued from page 143

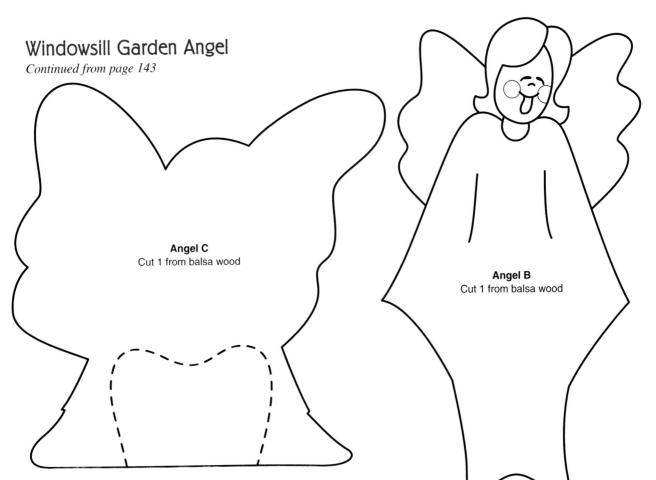

Angel C
Cut 1 from balsa wood

Angel B
Cut 1 from balsa wood

Angel A
Cut 1 from balsa wood

parts; let dry for 30 minutes and sand gently.

3. Hot-glue angel pieces together as shown, A atop B and B atop C (see Fig. 1, page 143).

Painting

1. *CD crate:* Using light foliage green, paint top edges of ends and bottom boards on sides; using sunbright yellow, paint ends; using purple dusk, paint handles and top boards on sides.

2. *Paint angel:* Using sunbright yellow, paint both layers of wings, including edges; using fleshtone, paint hands and feet, including edges; using buttermilk, paint gown, including edges; using territorial beige, paint angel's hair.

3. *Detail angel:* Using territorial beige, outline angel's wings, hands, feet and sections of gown; add details delineating lines and "folds" at knees. Using black, outline hair; add facial features. Add cheeks with pink parfait; color in open mouth with terra cotta.

4. *Halo:* Bend 2½" piece of wire into circle, twisting ends together in

a straight stem. Glue tail to back of angel's head.

5. *Stars:* Paint sunbright yellow; outline with territorial beige and add dots of territorial beige at star corners.

6. *Fence:* Paint all craft stick halves terra cotta; sand lightly to take a little paint off edges.

7. Using black paint, stencil "Garden Angel" on top slat of side, positioning words approximately 7½" from left edge and 5¼" from right edge. Loading liner with plenty of paint, paint over black lettering, leaving a little black showing along right and bottom edges of letters for "shading."

8. *Fence:* Wrap 16" piece of wire around craft stick about ½" from top and moving on to the next stick; repeat until all sticks are joined. Repeat with second 16" strand of wire, wrapping sticks about ½" from bottom. Bend wire ends to back and glue in place.

Assembly & Finishing

1. Glue fence to bottom board of crate in center. Glue angel so she is

sitting atop fence. Glue stars to crate as shown.

2. Drill holes for handle screws in ends of crate 1" below top edge. Screw handles to crate.

3. Following manufacturer's instructions, spray planter with several coats of matte-finish interior varnish. Place terra-cotta pots in planter. ✳

Earth Angels

Continued from page 144

2. Repeat steps 2–5 for Beautician Frame, cutting also one nurse hat from paper, painting and shading it as for other paper pieces, and spattering frame with thinned white paint.

3. Repeat steps 6–9 for Beautician Frame, writing "An Angel of a Nurse" in frame opening, and adding a cluster of tomato spice berries and forest green leaves to one side of nurse's hat.

4. Using craft glue, glue wings to frame front; hot-glue head over wings. Hot-glue Spanish moss hair to angel's head. Hot-glue hat to hair. Knot one small piece of fabric. Trim ends at an angle; hot-glue to center front of chin.

5. Repeat step 11 for Beautician Frame. ✳

Earth Angels Wings
Cut 1 from watercolor paper

Large Tree
Cut 1 from miracle sponge

Small Tree
Cut 1 from miracle sponge

Nurse Hat
Cut 1 from watercolor paper

Gingerbread Career Angels

Gingerbread Career Angels

4. Referring to "Color Choices," complete painting of gingerbread angels by filling in areas with color just as you would on a coloring book page.

5. When paints are dry, add outlines, facial features and other details—pleats, buttons, "lines" on paper, etc.—using either a #1 liner brush and black paint or fine-point textile marker.

6. Add lettering in center with black paint and liner brush or fabric marker.

7. Pour some calico red paint onto foam plate or palette. Referring to photo, dip heart-shaped sponge into paint and randomly stamp a border of hearts at various angles around gingerbread characters (hearts do not need to be evenly covered with red paint).

8. Using liner brush and black paint or fine-point textile marker throughout, outline each heart and add "stitches." Connect hearts with squiggly lines and add clusters of three tiny dots as desired to complete "frame."

Flock of Angels

1. Referring to patterns and following manufacturer's instructions, transfer desired design onto watercolor paper using transfer pen or pencil.

2. Using terra-cotta marker, paint face, arms and legs. Paint heart(s) red unless instructed otherwise. When colored areas are dry, add facial details with fine-point marking pen.

3. Referring to "Color Choices," finish coloring design, matching watercolor marker color to paint color and leaving white "highlight" areas uncolored. It is not necessary to color wings or any other areas which are "painted white."

4. When colored areas are dry, add outlines, facial features and other details—pleats, buttons, "lines" on paper, etc.—using fine-point marking pen.

5. Finish colored gingerbread angel to make desired project:

Magnet: Apply laminating sheet over front side of artwork; apply adhesive sheet to back of artwork. Peel protective sheet from adhesive and press artwork sticky side down on nonmagnetic side of magnetic sheeting. Cut out character. For an added feature, glue miniature clothespin to one hand for holding memos, notes, etc.

Key Chain: Apply laminating sheet to both sides of artwork. Cut out character. Punch hole near top center; attach key chain hardware through hole.

Pin: Apply laminating sheet to both sides of artwork. Cut out character. Glue pin back to back of character.

Hang Tags and Ornaments: Apply laminating sheet to both sides of artwork. Cut out character. Punch hole near top center. Insert wire ornament hanger hook or loop of decorative cord through hole.

Gift Tags: Apply adhesive sheet to back of artwork. Using paper edgers, cut around design so it is in center of 3" square of watercolor paper. Fold construction paper in half to make 4" square card. Peel protective sheet from adhesive and press design onto front of card. Punch hole in top corner near fold; thread loop of decorative cord or ribbon through hole. ✷

Catch a Falling Star Sweatshirt
Continued from page 148

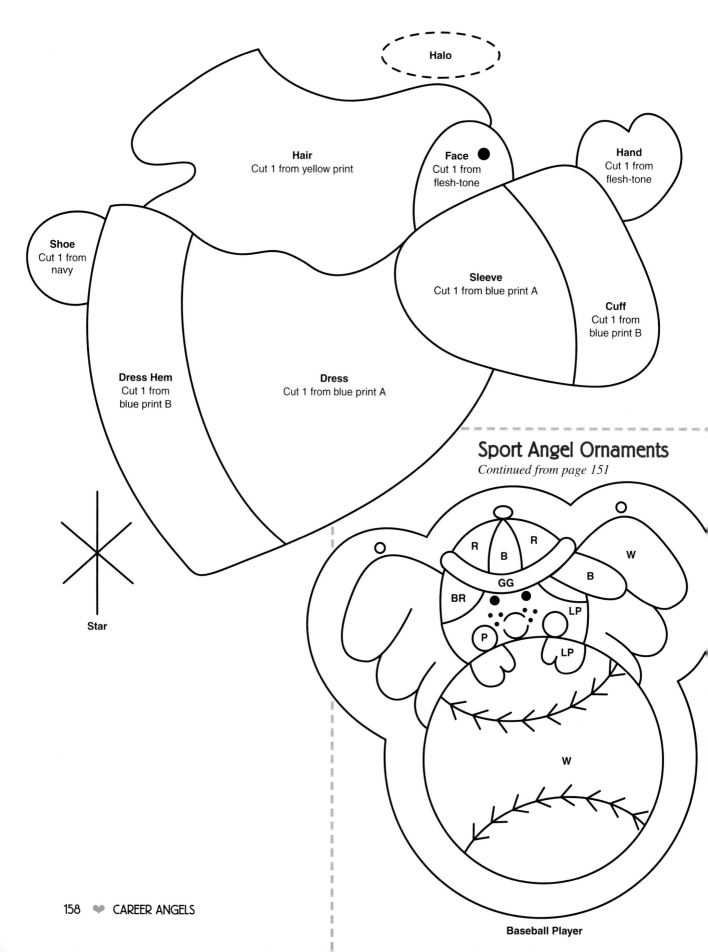

Halo

Hair
Cut 1 from yellow print

Face
Cut 1 from
flesh-tone

Hand
Cut 1 from
flesh-tone

Shoe
Cut 1 from
navy

Sleeve
Cut 1 from blue print A

Cuff
Cut 1 from
blue print B

Dress Hem
Cut 1 from
blue print B

Dress
Cut 1 from blue print A

Star

Sport Angel Ornaments
Continued from page 151

R   R
B
W
GG
B
BR
LP
P
LP
W

Baseball Player

Sport Angel Ornaments

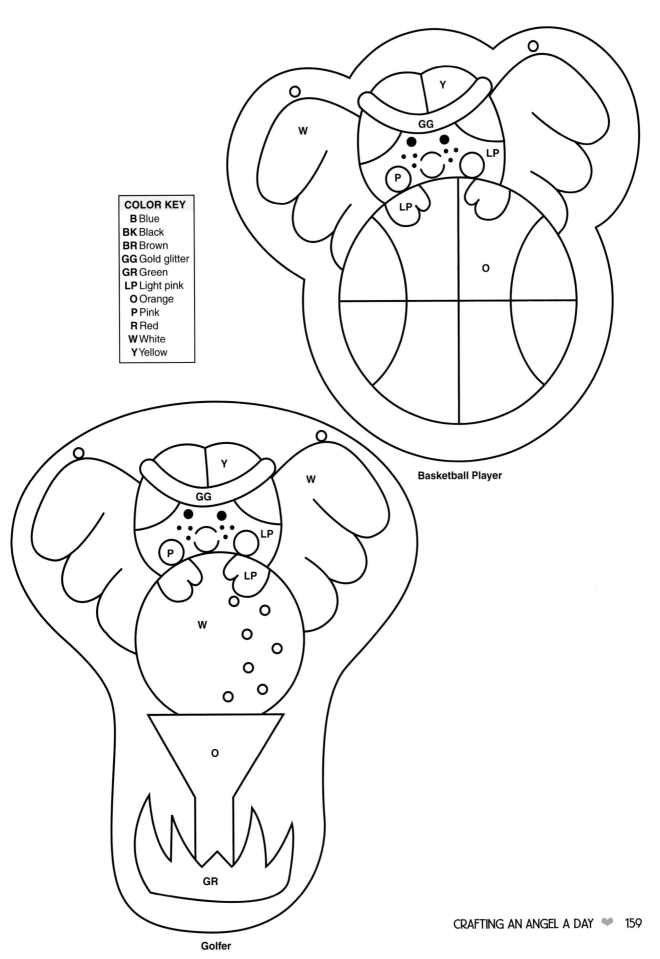

COLOR KEY
B Blue
BK Black
BR Brown
GG Gold glitter
GR Green
LP Light pink
O Orange
P Pink
R Red
W White
Y Yellow

Basketball Player

Golfer

With the whisper of winter's first snowfall comes extra care from angels. Bring these friendly snow angels, one and all, from the cold outdoors into your home!

Snow ANGELS

G ive your favorite birds their own special home decorated with their very own guardian angel!

Angelic Birdhouse

Design by Bonnie Stephens

Materials
- 4½" x 5" x 8¾" wooden birdhouse #11-2194 from Provo Craft
- 2¼" wooden circle cutout from Lara's Crafts
- Rusty Tin-Tiques from D&CC: 4¼" heart #24-7207-000
  4¾" snowman #24-7136-000
- Ceramcoat all-purpose sealer from Delta Technical Coatings
- Ceramcoat acrylic paints from Delta Technical Coatings:
  Terra cotta #2071
  Tomato spice #2098
  Medium flesh #2126
  Nightfall blue #2131
  White #2505
  Black #2506
- Ceramcoat satin interior varnish from Delta Technical Coatings
- Paintbrushes:
  ¾" flat
  10/0 liner
  Spatter brush
  Small stencil brush
- Stylus
- Dried Spanish moss
- 6" x 3½" piece Warm and Natural needled cotton from The Warm Co.
- Hand-sewing needle and off-white thread
- White 1" pompom
- Sprig of artificial greenery with red berries
- Strip of country-style plaid fabric
- Tacky craft glue
- Hot-glue gun
- Fine-grit sandpaper
- Tin snips
- Paper towels

Project Notes
Refer to photo throughout.

Let all paints, sealers, varnish, etc., dry between applications.

Use ¾" flat brush unless instructed otherwise.

Painting
1. Sand birdhouse lightly; apply a coat of all-purpose sealer. Sand again.

2. Paint birdhouse tomato spice; paint roof nightfall blue. Paint wooden circle medium flesh for angel's face.

3. Dot eyes onto angel's face using stylus dipped in black paint. Redip stylus before making second eye so both are the same size.

4. For cheeks, dip stencil brush in tomato spice. Rub most of paint off onto paper towels, then scrub face in a circular motion with nearly dry brush to make cheeks.

5. Add mouth using liner brush dipped in thinned tomato spice.

6. Dip flat brush in white; wipe off excess paint onto paper towel, then lightly brush tin snowman leaving hat unpainted. Referring to step 3, add eyes, mouth and buttons with stylus dipped in black. Using liner brush, paint nose with terra cotta.

Assembly & Finishing
1. Cut tin heart in half down center to make wings. Using tacky glue through step 2, glue wings, curved side down, to front roof edge on birdhouse. Using spatter brush and thinned white paint, lightly spatter wings and front of birdhouse.

2. Glue angel's head atop wings; glue snowman at bottom left of birdhouse.

3. Coat entire piece with one or two coats of satin interior varnish.

4. Using hot-glue gun throughout, glue Spanish moss hair to angel's head.

5. With needle and thread, make hat by seaming short edges of needled cotton together to make a tube. Run gathering stitch around one edge of tube; gather tightly and knot. Turn hat inside out so seam and gathered edge are inside; fold up ½" cuff around bottom of hat.

6. Glue hat to head with seam in back. Glue pompom to top of hat. Tuck greenery into hat cuff and glue in place.

7. Knot strip of fabric or tie in a bow; trim ends as desired and glue at angel's neck, slightly left of center. ✳

Hang this pair of winsome ornaments around your house, or even from your car's rear-view mirror for winter fun!

Snowmen Pocket Ornaments

Design by Angie Wilhite

Materials
Each Ornament
♥ Fabrics:
  4" square gold
  3" square blue plaid
♥ Felt:
  4" x 8" denim blue
  4" square off-white
♥ Pellon products:
  4" square Sof-Shape fusible interfacing
  4" square Heavy-Duty Wonder-Under fusible transfer web
  4" square Craft-Bond
  4" square Fusible Fleece
  4" square Wonder-Under fusible transfer web
♥ Metallic gold fine thread
♥ 6-strand embroidery floss: cream, orange and denim blue
♥ Denim blue sewing thread
♥ Hand-sewing needle
♥ 8" piece (⅛"-wide) cream satin ribbon
♥ Fabric glue
♥ Iron

Project Notes
Refer to photo throughout for placement.

Use 2 strands floss or metallic thread for all embroidery and blanket stitch.

Instructions
1. Launder and dry fabrics without using fabric softener.

2. Following manufacturer's instructions, fuse interfacing to backs of blue plaid and gold fabrics. Next, fuse heavy-duty transfer web to back of gold fabric, and Craft-Bond to back of blue plaid fabric. Fuse fleece then transfer web to back of off-white felt.

3. Referring to patterns (page 182), cut snowman from off-white felt and wings from gold. Cut two pocket shapes from denim blue felt; cut one star and one piece ⅜" x 1" for bow tie from blue plaid fabric.

4. To gather center of bow tie, sew gathering stitch down center of ⅜"x 1"

rectangle with denim thread. Pull thread to gather fabric and wrap thread twice around center of bow tie; knot on back of tie.

5. Fuse wings, then snowman to front of one denim blue felt pocket. Blanket stitch around wings with metallic gold thread. Using denim blue floss, blanket stitch around snowman and add two French knot eyes. Using orange embroidery floss, add nose with two ⅛" straight stitches.

6. Using cream embroidery floss, blanket stitch across top of pocket front; holding both felt pockets together, wrong sides facing, blanket stitch down one side, across bottom and up other side.

7. Glue ends of ribbon inside corners of pocket for hanger. Glue plaid star at one corner and glue bow tie to snowman. ✳

Pattern on page 182

H

ere's an original gift for someone you love–a keepsake pillow declaring your affection!

"Melt My Heart" Pillow

Design by Chris Malone

Materials

- Coordinating woven fabrics:
  - 1/2 yard blue plaid
  - 1/3 yard tea-bag osnaburg
  - 1" x 44" strip red print or stripe
  - 5" x 10" piece white-on-white print A
  - 3" x 6" piece white-on-white print B
  - Scrap of red print
  - Scrap of orange print
- 6-strand embroidery floss: black and white
- Tapestry needle
- Fusible web
- 2 (3mm) black beads
- 12" square knife-edge pillow form or polyester fiberfill
- Air- or water-soluble fabric marking pen
- Embroidery hoop
- Hand-sewing needle and blue thread
- Seam sealant
- Fabric glue
- Iron

Project Notes

All piecing is done with right sides of fabrics facing. Measurements include ¼" seam allowance.

Border strips are cut long and trimmed later to allow for individual differences in piecing.

All embroidery is done with 2 strands floss.

Pillow Front

1. Mark 8½" square in center of osnaburg; cut out, cutting approximately ½" outside line.

2. Referring to pattern (page 180) and using air-soluble pen, write "You Melt My Heart" and draw snowflakes on osnaburg.

3. Place fabric in embroidery hoop. Backstitch letters with black embroidery floss, adding French knots at ends of each letter. Using white floss, straight stitch each snowflake with stitches radiating from center point; add French knot in center of each snowflake and at end of each straight stitch.

4. Following manufacturer's instructions, fuse a 5" square of fusible web onto one half of wrong side of white print A. Peel off paper backing; fold other half of fabric over onto web and fuse layers together.

5. Fuse additional web to wrong sides of white print B, orange and red prints, and to one side of fused white print A. Referring to patterns (page 180), cut body and head from doubled white print A, wings from white print B, heart from red print and nose from orange print. Following manufacturer's instructions, fuse appliqués in place on osnaburg.

6. Using black floss throughout, sew 3mm beads in place for eyes; straight stitch eyebrows and back-stitch smile.

Assembly & Finishing

1. Trim pillow front to marked 8½" square. Sew red strip to one side of block; trim even. Repeat on other side, then top and bottom.

2. From blue plaid, cut two 2" x 30" strips; sew to red border on all sides as in step 1. Press seams to outside.

3. From remaining blue plaid, cut two 12½" x 8" rectangles for pillow back. Press under ¼" hem along one long edge of each rectangle; fold hem over again and sew in place.

4. Lay pillow front right side up on work surface. Place one back piece on top of front, right sides facing, matching unfinished long edge to top edge of pillow front. Repeat with second back piece, aligning unfinished edge with bottom of pillow front; hemmed edges will overlap. Pin in place; sew backs to pillow front. Trim corners; turn pillow cover right side out. Insert pillow insert through hemmed opening.

5. From remaining plaid fabric, cut 1" x 5" strip; fringe ½" on each short end. Apply seam sealant to long edges; let dry. Tie knot in center of strip; glue knot on left side of snowman's neckline. ✱

Pattern on page 180

This friendly angel has generously offered a winter hideaway for the birds! Craft him to add warmth to your winter home!

Snow Angel for the Birds

Design by Veleta Stafney

Materials
- Styrofoam plastic foam shapes:
  5" ball
  3" ball
  2 (2½") eggs
- ⅜" wooden furniture button
- Ceramcoat acrylic paints from Delta Technical Coatings:
  Adobe red #2046
  Light ivory #2401
  Bright red #2503
  White #2505
  Black #2506
- Ceramcoat Decorative Snow snow paste #31-002-0400 from Delta Technical Coatings
- ½" flat paintbrush
- Stylus
- 3½" black felt hat
- 4" grapevine wreath
- 5 yards jute twine
- Dark green 6-strand embroidery floss
- 2 (⅜") flat burgundy buttons
- 1½" x 18" strip multicolored flannel fabric
- Small amount of green sheet moss
- 2 (1") mushroom birds
- Craft stick
- Paper towels
- Low-melt glue gun

Project Notes
Refer to photo throughout for placement.

Let all glue and paints dry between applications.

Instructions
1. *Body:* Flatten sides of plastic foam shapes by pressing one side of 3" ball (head), opposite sides of 5" ball (body) and larger end of each egg (arm) against a smooth, hard surface. Paint all pieces light ivory. Glue flattened side of head to one flattened side of body; glue flattened ends of arms to body as shown.

2. *Face:* Paint furniture button bright red for nose. Glue nose to center of face area. Using stylus dipped in black, dot on eyes and five mouth dots, redipping before each

dot so all are the same size. Dip brush into adobe red; paint on paper towel until almost no paint remains in brush. Blush cheeks with nearly dry brush. Using stylus and white, add tiny highlight dot to each cheek and comma stroke to nose.

3. *Hat:* Glue hat to top of head; dent side of hat lightly. Carefully uncoil grapevine wreath; break off two coils and wrap around brim of hat. Wrap two or three coils around body.

4. *Wings:* Cut five 1-yard pieces of jute. Holding them together as one piece, tie into a large bow and glue to back of neck; trim ends.

5. *Buttons:* Cut two 4" lengths dark green floss; thread though buttonholes from back. Tie floss ends in a bow on front of each button; trim

ends. Glue buttons to body.

6. *Scarf:* Fray all edges ¼" on fabric strip. Tie around snowman's neck, positioning knot to one side. Glue scarf ends to snowman as desired.

7. *Birds and nests:* Glue small amount of sheet moss to left front edge of hat brim and top of right arm. Glue bird to each nest.

8. *Snow:* Using craft stick, apply snow paste to hat, nests, birds, scarf, wreath and snowman. ❈

Project Notes

Let all finishes, paints and ink dry between applications.

Refer to photo throughout for color choices and placement.

Instructions

1. Tape off an even border of about ½" all around wood slice.

2. Mix equal amounts of French blue paint and glazing medium and base-coat center of wood slice with mixture.

3. Referring to pattern (page 181), paint snow with winter white and icy white, adding a bit of French blue shading as desired.

4. Paint melted snowman in foreground; add his scarf with cobalt blue, his buttons with red light, and his stick arms with a mixture of burnt sienna and raw umber. Using liner brush, add some tufts of grass.

5. Using the snowman as a guide for positioning, paint wings on plaque with pearl white, shading lightly with a little autumn leaves.

6. Paint sun medium yellow, shading with autumn leaves; add rays with medium yellow.

7. Using .3mm marking pen, add details, outlining, etc.

8. Base-coat snowman cutout on all surfaces with winter white; shade with a little French blue. Add cobalt blue scarf, red light buttons, autumn leaves "carrot" nose and black eyes. Add details, including tiny X's for mouth, with .3mm marking pen. Glue snowman to plaque over wings; glue twig arms at his sides; draw halo with gold leafing pen.

9. Base-coat tree cutouts on all surfaces with Hauser green dark. Add crisscross patterns to fronts of trees using desired combination of red light, medium yellow, French blue and gold. Glue trees to plaque as shown.

The next time your little ones ask what happens to snowmen, you can share this heartwarming plaque with them!

All Snowmen Go to Heaven

Design by Barbara A. Woolley

Materials

- Oval wood slice with bark, about 9" x 6"
- Wooden cutouts:
  2"-tall snowman
  3 (2") pine trees
- 2 (1½") wooden twigs
- 20" piece (16-gauge) rusty or black wire
- Folk Art acrylic paints from Plaid Enterprises:
  Winter white #429
  Medium yellow #455
  Hauser green dark #461
  Raw umber #485
  Red light #629
  French blue #639
  Pearl white #659
  Icy white #701
  Cobalt blue #720
  Autumn leaves #920
  Burnt sienna #943
- Folk Art glazing medium #693 from Plaid Enterprises
- Blend gel #867 from Plaid Enterprises
- Matte acrylic sealer #788 from Plaid Enterprises
- 18-karat gold leafing pen from Krylon
- Zig Woodcraft .6mm black marking pen
- Zig Millennium .3mm black pen
- Spatter brush or an old toothbrush
- Paintbrushes: Liner #3 and #12 round
- Masking tape
- Craft drill with small bit
- Craft cement

Continued on page 181

Pick out scraps of brightly colored felt to craft this whimsical angel ornament!

Let It Snow Ornament

Design by Chris Malone

Materials

- Felt:
  9" x 12" sheet each white and gold
  Small pieces red, bright green, blue and black
- Black 6-strand embroidery floss
- Tapestry needle
- Polyester fiberfill
- 2 (3mm) black beads
- 2 (2") forked twigs
- 8" piece ¼"-wide red grosgrain ribbon
- Pea-size ball of orange oven-dry modeling clay
- ¾" plastic bone ring
- Craft cement
- Oven

Project Note

Refer to photo throughout for placement.

Instructions

1. Referring to patterns (page 182), cut pieces from felt: two bodies from white, two sets of wings from gold, four mittens from red, two buttons from bright green, cut four boots from black and one scarf plus one ⅜" x 5" strip from blue.

2. Using 2 strands of black floss throughout, blanket stitch scarf front to neckline of one snowman.

Referring to pattern for placement throughout, sew bead eyes to snowman's face; straight stitch eyebrows and backstitch smile.

3. Blanket stitch boot halves together to make two boots, leaving tops open; stuff lightly with fiberfill.

4. Pin snowman front and back together, wrong sides facing, with tops of boots sandwiched between halves. Join all around with blanket stitch, catching boots in stitching and stuffing snowman lightly before closing.

5. Join wings with blanket stitch all around; glue to back of snowman.

6. Blanket stitch around blue strip and around both buttons. Add two French knots in center of each button. Glue buttons down center of snowman. Tie knot in middle of blue strip and glue knot to scarf on left side of neckline.

7. Glue twig arms to snowman.

8. Blanket stitch mitten halves together to make two mittens, leaving tops open. Overlap mittens and glue together.

9. Cut ribbon into 2" and 6" pieces. Fold 2" piece in half; glue ends to back of top mitten. Tie remaining ribbon in a bow; notch ribbon ends. Glue bow to top of mitten. Hang mittens over fork of right twig arm; secure with cement.

10. For nose, roll orange clay into a cone; flatten broad end on a hard, smooth surface. Bake nose in oven, following manufacturer's instructions; cool. Cement flat end to face.

11. Sew ring to back of head for hanger. ✳

Patterns on page 182

L iven up your Christmas party with this pair of cheery snow angels! Everyone will love their soft, puffy bodies, colorful outfits and happy personalities!

Snow Angel Couple

Design by Veleta Stafney

Materials
Both Snow People

- Woodsies wooden products from Forster Inc:
  - 4 jumbo craft sticks
  - 2 large (1¼") circles
  - 2 doll stands
  - Medium (⅞") square
  - 2 medium (1½") ovals
  - Medium (¾") circle
  - Small (⅞") star
- 2 (3"-wide x ¼"-thick) wooden heart cutouts
- 2 (¼") wooden furniture buttons
- ¼ yard white #550 Rainbow Plush Felt from Kunin Felt
- Americana acrylic paints from DecoArt:
  - Titanium white #DA1
  - Peaches 'n cream #DA23
  - Lamp black #DA67
  - Napa red #DA165
  - Primary red #DA199
  - Primary yellow #DA201
- ¼" flat paintbrush
- Old paintbrush
- Stylus
- Americana satin-finish acrylic varnish #DS15 from DecoArt
- Glimmer #DHM3 Heavy Metals liquid fabric glitter from DecoArt
- Glamour Dust ultra-fine glitter #DAS37 from DecoArt
- ¼ yard red Christmas print fabric
- 3 (¾") flat red buttons
- Yellow 6-strand embroidery floss
- 2 (2" x 5¼") sets puffy white angel wings
- 5" imitation candy cane
- Extra-fine–point permanent marking pens: white and black
- Polyester fiberfill
- Tacky craft glue
- Hand-sewing needle and white thread
- Sewing machine (optional)
- Paper towels

Project Notes

Follow instructions for Basic Snowman for each; add finishing details as directed for Mr. Snowman and Mrs. Snowman.

Let all glue, paints, inks and finishes dry between applications.

Use ¼" flat paintbrush unless instructed otherwise.

Basic Snowman

1. *Armature and head:* Overlap two jumbo craft sticks by 1"; glue together. Trim off one end in a straight line (this will be bottom edge of body). For head, glue top half of wooden circle cutout to top of rounded end of body.

2. Paint assembled body and head titanium white. Using black marking pen, draw dot-dash lines down center and both sides of body to define legs.

3. Referring to Fig. 1, glue doll stand to center of wooden heart. Paint both pieces lamp black. Using white pen, draw "stitching lines" around edge of heart; draw "shoelaces" in centers of rounded lobes of heart. Coat doll stand and heart with varnish.

Fig. 1

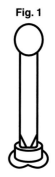

4. Fill opening in doll stand with glue to depth of ¾". Gently push bottom (flat) edge of body into glue; hold in place until it is secure.

5. *Face:* Paint furniture button Napa red for nose; glue to middle of face. Using stylus dipped in black, dot on eyes and five mouth dots, redipping before each dot so all are the same size. Draw eyelashes and mouth line with black extra-fine-point pen. Dip brush into peaches 'n cream; paint on paper towel until almost no paint remains in brush. Blush cheeks with nearly dry brush. Using stylus and titanium white, add a tiny white highlight dot to each cheek and comma stroke to nose.

6. *Body:* Referring to pattern (page 183), cut two bodies from white plush felt. With right sides facing, sew pieces together along curved edges. Turn body right side out.

7. Sew gathering stitch around both openings. Place body over wooden head, positioning seams at sides. Pull gathers tightly at top to secure body at neck. Knot thread; spot-glue to secure.

8. Lightly stuff body through open bottom with fiberfill. Pull bottom gathering thread tightly around legs; knot and spot-glue.

9. *Arms:* Cut 4" x 10" strip white plush felt. Fold in half lengthwise, right sides facing, and sew together along long edges. Turn tube right side out.

10. Wrap center of arm tube tightly with white thread; knot. Lightly stuff each arm through open end. Overlap open ends of arms ¼"; sew gathering stitch through all layers and pull tightly to close; knot. Place arms over head; glue ends to back of neck.

Mr. Snowman Details

1. *Hat:* Glue medium wooden square to upper half of medium wooden oval (Fig. 2). Paint lamp black. Draw stitching lines around brim and along crown with white marking pen. Varnish hat. Glue hat to front of head, tilting it to one side as shown.

Fig. 2

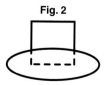

2. Paint star primary yellow; draw stitching line around edges with

black pen. Varnish star. Glue star to crown of hat.

3. *Scarf:* Tear 12" x ¾" strip of fabric; tie around snowman's neck, positioning knot to one side

4. Using yellow embroidery floss, sew one button to snowman's body just below head, and other two down center of body below arms.

5. *Bow at feet:* Tear 1½" x 12" strip fabric; tie in a bow and glue to base of feet at top of doll stand.

6. Glue wings to back of arms.

7. Using old paintbrush, brush liquid

Continues on page 183

Digging through your craft closet is half the fun of putting this festive tree together! Each adorable angel is made from old spools, scraps of fabric and ribbon, wooden beads and Spanish moss!

Angel Tree

Design by Bonnie Stephens

Materials

- Wooden products from WoodWorks:
  Ornament tree #OT-1600
  Little People girl #LP-4040
  Doll pin body #CP-R375
  Large (13/4"-tall x 1½"-diameter) spool
  3 small (1¼"-tall x ⅞"-diameter) spools
  1½"-tall x 1⅜"-wide candle cup
  1½" heart cutout
  3 (1") ball knobs
  ¾" ball knob
  1¾"-square chalkboard
- Ceramcoat acrylic paints from Delta Technical Coatings:
  Forest green #2010
  Burnt umber #2025
  Tomato spice #2098
  Medium flesh #2126
  White #2505
  Black #2506
- Butter cream #2523
- Paintbrushes:
  ¾" flat
  10/0 liner
  Spatter brush
  Small stencil brush
- Stylus
- Paint palette
- Assorted fabric scraps including natural muslin
- 3" strip (½"–1") crochet edging or lace
- Hand-sewing needle and matching threads
- Natural raffia
- 12" piece jute twine
- 12" piece (⅛"-wide) red satin ribbon
- 3" cinnamon stick
- Dried Spanish moss
- 20-gauge wire
- Craft drill and small bit
- Tacky craft glue
- Hot-glue gun

Project Notes

Refer to photo throughout.

Use ¾" flat paintbrush unless instructed otherwise.

Let all paints dry between coats.

Use tacky craft glue to assemble tree and to glue wooden ball knobs, candle cups, spools and heart cutout together. Use glue gun for all other gluing.

Painting

1. Base-coat wooden pieces on all surfaces as follows: *head of wooden girl, head of doll pin and all ball knobs*—medium flesh; *candle cup and one small spool*—forest green; *body of doll pin and large spool*—tomato spice; *two small spools, body of wooden girl and doll cutout*—butter cream.

2. Add faces to all ball knobs and to heads on doll pin and wooden girl shape:

Eyes: Dip stylus in black paint; dot once on palette and touch to head. Repeat for second eye.

Cheeks: Dip stencil brush into tomato spice; scrub on paper towel until almost no paint remains in brush. Scrub cheeks in a circular motion with nearly dry brush.

Mouths: Thin a little tomato spice paint with water. Using 10/0 liner brush or stylus, paint or dot tiny mouth onto each head.

3. Thin a little burnt umber paint with water. Paint all surfaces of tree and chalkboard frame.

4. Glue components of tree together. Using thinned white paint and spatter brush, lightly spatter tree and all painted pieces.

Angels

1. Drill small hole in top of each angel head; bend six 2" pieces of wire into hanging loops and glue straight ends in holes.

2. *Doll-pin angel:* Tie jute twine into a bow; trim ends and glue bow to back of angel for wings. Cut a 2" square of fabric; run a gathering stitch across one edge with needle and thread; pull to gather to about 1"; knot. Glue gathered edge ½" below neckline. Paint black "feet" on fronts of tomato spice "legs."

3. *Candle-cup angel:* Glue 1" ball knob head to base of candle cup. Tie 6" piece of red ribbon in a bow; trim ends and glue bow at back of neckline for wings. Glue scraps of Spanish moss to head for hair. Tie knot in the middle of a ½"-wide strip of fabric; trim ends at an angle and glue atop hair at base of hanger.

4. *Wooden-girl angel:* Tie 6" piece of red ribbon in a bow; glue at angel's neckline. Using liner brush and thinned white paint, paint "Let It Snow" on chalkboard; glue angel to front left edge of chalkboard

frame. Glue scraps of Spanish moss hair to head; add a "hair bow" made from a tiny knotted strip of fabric.

5. *Butter-cream spool angel:* Glue butter-cream spools end to end; glue 1" ball knob head to one end. Cut a 2" square of fabric; run a gathering stitch across one edge with needle and thread; pull to gather to about 1"; knot. Glue gathered edge at neckline. Glue crocheted edging around neckline; trim off excess. Tear a 1" strip of natural muslin; tie in a simple bow for wings; trim ends and glue to back of body. Glue

scraps of Spanish moss hair to head.

6. *Large spool angel:* Glue 1" ball knob head to end of tomato spice spool. Tear 1"-wide strip of fabric for wings; tie knot in middle, trim ends, and glue to back of spool. Tie knot in a tiny strip of fabric; trim ends and glue to top of spool below angel's mouth. Glue Spanish moss hair to head.

7. *Forest green spool angel:* Using liner brush and thinned black paint, draw "stitching line" around edge of wooden heart cutout; glue heart to one end of small forest green spool

for collar, with point of heart facing front. Glue ¾" ball knob head atop heart. Glue cinnamon stick to heart behind head for wings. Tie knot in a tiny strip of fabric; trim ends and glue to top of heart below angel's mouth. Glue Spanish moss hair to head.

Final Assembly

1. Knot strip of fabric around tree trunk at base.

2. Tie each angel's hanging loop to "branch" of ornament tree with raffia bow. Top bows with a touch of tacky glue to hold securely. ✳

Even beginner painters will have success crafting this charming hand-painted angel pillow.

Snow Angel Pillow

Design by June Fiechter

Materials

- 💜 2 (13") squares heavy off-white fabric
- 💜 Polyester fiberfill or foam pillow form
- 💜 Ceramcoat acrylic paints from Delta Technical Coatings:
  Spice brown #2049
  Wedgwood blue #2069
  Mendocino red #2406
  Leprechaun #2422
  Black #2506
  Dark goldenrod #2519
  Pine green #2526
- 💜 Ceramcoat textile medium #10- 300-0201 from Delta Technical Coatings
- 💜 Crafters Pick Jewel Bond glue by API
- 💜 Diamond Dust multicolor fine glitter from Creative Beginnings
- 💜 9 (10") pieces pearl #032 fine (#8) metallic braid from Kreinik Mfg. Co. Inc.
- 💜 4 (½" x 10") torn fabric strips to match red and green paints
- 💜 Paintbrushes
- 💜 Matching sewing thread and hand-sewing needle
- 💜 Sewing machine (optional)
- 💜 Iron

Project Notes

Refer to photo throughout for placement.

Before painting, mix all colors with textile medium following manufacturer's instructions.

Painting

1. Referring to pattern (page 184), transfer design to center of one piece of off-white fabric.

2. Shade outer edges of snowdrifts and snowman with Wedgwood blue. Then, thin a little of the Wedgwood blue mixture with a little water. With this thinned mixture, continue to shade along inside of undiluted Wedgwood shading. This thinned mixture will "bleed" on fabric, so keep away from the edges.

3. Using Mendocino red, paint hat, coat and holly berries near snowdrifts.

4. Using pine green, paint scarf, bow and band on hat, patches on jacket and trees.

5. Using leprechaun, paint holly leaves.

6. Using spice brown, paint tree trunk and branch "arms."

7. Using dark goldenrod, paint carrot nose.

8. Using black, paint eyes; outline snow angel and snowdrifts.

9. When all paints are thoroughly dry, paint over wings and shaded edges of snowdrifts with glue. Sprinkle with fine glitter. Let glue dry undisturbed for 24 hours, then shake off excess glitter.

Assembly

1. Sew fabric squares together along three sides, right sides facing. Turn right side out; iron edges.

2. Cut one piece of braid in half; holding pieces together, tie in a small double bow. Glue bow to snowman's neckline.

3. Stuff pillow; sew opening closed by hand.

4. Lay two pieces fine (#8) metallic braid atop one fabric strip. Holding fabric and braid together, tie in a bow around a cluster of fabric on one corner of pillow. Add a drop of glue to hold fabric and braid in place. Repeat with remaining fabric strips and braid. ✳

Pattern on page 184

With his big heart, rosy cheeks and tangled-up stars, this wooden painted angel will add a bright touch to your Christmas tree!

Snowman with Heart Ornament

Design by Chris Malone

Materials
- Wooden cutouts:
  6"-tall primitive snowman
  4" x 3" wings
  1/2" x 1" primitive heart
  1 1/4" star
  2 (7/16") stars
- Aerosol sealer/finish
- Americana acrylic paints from DecoArt:
  Antique gold #DA9
  Cadmium orange #DA14
  Raspberry #DA28
  Williamsburg blue #DA40
  Jade green #DA57
  Lamp black #DA67
  Light buttermilk #DA164
  Golden straw #DA168
- Fine-grit sandpaper
- Paintbrushes:
  Small flat
  Round
  Stencil brush
- Fine-point black permanent marking pen
- 24" piece (19-gauge) black wire
- Craft drill and small bit
- Craft glue
- Paper towels

Project Notes
Refer to photo throughout.

Let all finishes, paints and ink dry between applications.

Instructions
1. Drill small hole in top of each wing. Sand all wooden cutouts; spray with sealer.

2. Using flat paintbrush, base-coat all surfaces of wooden cutouts: *snowman*—light buttermilk; *wings*—a half-and-half mixture of light buttermilk and Williamsburg blue; *heart*—raspberry; *1 1/4" star*—antique gold; *7/16" stars*—golden straw.

3. Referring to pattern (page 180), dip handle of paintbrush into black paint and dot on one eye; repeat for second eye.

4. Dip stencil brush in raspberry; brush most of paint off onto paper towel, then tap nearly dry brush on cheeks.

5. Using round brush, paint carrot nose with cadmium orange and scarf with jade green. When dry, add squiggly stripes of light buttermilk to scarf.

6. Add details and outlines with fine-point marking pen. Spray on another coat of finish.

7. Glue wings to back of snowman and heart to front.

8. For hanger, poke one end of wire through hole in one wing from back to front. Wrap end around rest of wire to hold; curl wire end around pencil or paintbrush handle. Continue to randomly curl wire, wrapping it once or twice around each wooden star. Poke remaining end through hole in other wing and secure in the same manner as the first. ✳

Pattern on page 180

With her pine-bough wings and wreath and fiberfill-and-grapevine body, this delightful angel carries oodles of sweet country charm wherever she goes!

Country Snow Angel

Design by Veleta Stafney

Materials
- Clean, dry 24-ounce soda bottle with cap, label removed
- 1½" wooden ball knob
- ¼" wooden furniture button
- Woodsies wooden cutouts from Forster Inc:
  2 large (1⅜") stars
  Medium (1¼") star
  2 small (⅞") stars
- ½ yard Warm and Natural Batting from The Warm Company
- 2½ cups plastic doll pellets
- Polyester fiberfill
- 6" grapevine wreath
- Americana acrylic paints fromDecoArt:
  Titanium white #DA1
  Lamp black #DA67
  Coral rose #DA103
  True red #DA129
  Light buttermilk #DA164
  Primary yellow #DA201
- Americana satin-finish acrylic varnish #DS15 from DecoArt
- Snow-Tex decorative snow paste #DAS9 from DecoArt
- Glamour Dust ultra-fine glitter #DAS37 from DecoArt
- Woven burgundy plaid fabric:
  1½" x 14½" strip
  3¼" x 7½" strip
- 4 (12") stems imitation greenery
- 3 (⅞") flat tortoise-shell buttons
- Red 6-strand embroidery floss
- ¼" flat paintbrush
- Stylus
- Toothpick
- Fine-point black permanent marking pen
- Hand-sewing needle and cream thread
- Craft cement
- Fabric glue
- Paper towels

Project Notes
Refer to photo throughout for placement.

Let all glue, paints, inks and finishes dry between applications.

Using fabric glue unless otherwise indicated.

Basic Snowman
1. *Body and head:* Pour 1 cup doll pellets into soda bottle; glue lid onto bottle. Using craft cement, glue wooden ball knob to top of lid.

2. *Face:* Paint wooden ball knob light buttermilk. Paint furniture button true red for nose; using craft cement, glue nose to middle of face. Using stylus dipped in black, dot on eyes and five mouth dots, redipping before each dot so all are the same size. Draw eyelashes with black fine-point pen. Dip brush into coral rose; paint on paper towel until almost no paint remains in brush. Blush cheeks with nearly dry brush. Using stylus and titanium white, add tiny white highlight dots to cheeks and comma stroke to nose. Varnish head.

3. *Body:* Cut one piece batting 14¼" x 19". Right sides facing, sew 14¼" edges together leaving 2½" opening in center. Turn right side out. Sew gathering stitch around both ends of tube. Pull thread tight on one end to close; knot. This will be body bottom.

4. Liberally apply glue to bottom of bottle, spreading it to edges. Insert bottle into body through open end; press firmly onto bottom. Pull gathers of open end tightly around neck. Knot; spot-glue to secure.

5. Through 2½" opening in seam, pour rest of pellets into body and stuff body lightly with fiberfill. Sew or glue opening closed.

6. Sew a gathering stitch around body 3" below neck. Pull up gathers slightly and knot thread.

7. Carefully unwind grapevine wreath; wrap wreath around body three times.

8. *Arms:* Cut 5" x 18" strip batting. Fold in half lengthwise, right sides facing, and sew together along long edges. Turn tube right side out. Tie tube in a knot, positioning knot in center. Lightly stuff each arm through open end. Overlap open ends of arms ¼"; sew gathering stitch through all layers and pull tightly to close; knot. Place arms over head; glue sewn ends to back of neck. Glue knot to body as shown.

Finishing

1. *Scarf:* Fray all edges ¼" on 14½" fabric strip. Tie around snowman's neck, positioning knot to one side; glue scarf ends to snowman's arm.

2. *Hat:* Fray ¼" on both long sides of 7½" fabric strip. Fold up one long edge for cuff; glue. Glue cuff edge of hat around head with opening in back, trimming off excess fabric. Wrap floss around hat 1¼" from top to close tightly; knot and trim thread ends.

3. *Wings:* Lay three greenery stems side by side; twist together in center. Glue center to back of arms; bend out stems on each side to resemble wings.

4. *Wreath:* Bend remaining greenery stem into 3" circle; glue to body over hands.

5. Using red embroidery floss, sew one button to snowman's body below head, and other two to body between strands of wreath.

6. Paint stars primary yellow; draw stitching line around edges with black pen. Glue small star to one end of scarf; glue small and medium stars to wreath; glue large and medium stars to bottom of body.

7. Using toothpick, apply snow paste to wings, hat, scarf, wreath, body and stars. Sprinkle generously with ultra-fine glitter; shake off excess and let dry. ✳

W

elcome friends and family into your home with this colorful door decoration featuring a friendly snow angel bundled up for winter!

Cool Christmas Door Decor

Design by Joyce Atwood

Materials
- ♥ Americana acrylic paints from DecoArt:
  Buttermilk #DA3
  Burnt orange #DA16
  Spice pink #DA30
  Lamp black #DA67
  Napa red #DA165
  Payne's grey #DA167
  Wisteria #DA211
  Deep periwinkle #DA212
  Admiral blue #DA213
  Peony pink #DA215
- ♥ Glamour dust #DAS37 ultra-fine glitter from DecoArt
- ♥ Royal paintbrushes:
  ⁵⁄₁₆" stencil brush #SB-1
  ⅜" angle Aqualon #2160
- #6 Langnickel #5005 Royal sable
- #16 Langnickel #5005 Royal sable
- #0 liner #595
- #4 Aqualon #2250 ¼ angle #160
- #6 Aqualon #2150-8
- ♥ Decorative wooden window frame or cabinet-door front panel, approximately 13" x 21½"
- ♥ ¼" plywood
- ♥ Craft saw
- ♥ Sandpaper
- ♥ Tack cloth
- ♥ Wood glue or hot-glue gun
- ♥ Aerosol matte-finish varnish
- ♥ Sawtooth hanger

Project Notes
Refer to photo throughout for assembly and color placement.

Using photocopier with enlarging capabilities, enlarge snowman pattern 154 percent before cutting.

Let all paints dry between coats and applications and before applying adjacent colors unless instructed otherwise.

Surface Preparation
1. Referring to patterns (pages 185 and 186), cut snowman, nose, feet, star and two mittens from ¼" plywood; cut also one 6" x 2½" rectangle for sign. Sand pieces lightly; wipe off dust with tack cloth.

2. Applying paint to front surface and edges throughout, base-coat frame and wooden cutouts: *hat and mittens (reverse one mitten before painting)*—peony pink ; *coat area*—deep periwinkle; *head, wings, body bottom and feet, star and sign*—buttermilk; *nose*—burnt orange; *scarf area and frame*—admiral blue.

3. Base-coat back surface of entire snowman with buttermilk.

Painting & Detailing
1. Paint wings with a second coat of buttermilk; shake glitter over wings while paint is still wet.

2. Using deep periwinkle, shade around face, entire bottom of body and feet. Using admiral blue, shade wings all around. Using Napa red, shade nose and, using liner, add some detail lines across surface of carrot. Highlight center of nose with a very light dry-brush of buttermilk.

3. Stipple cheeks with a light application of Napa red. Using wooden tip of paintbrush handle dipped in lamp black, dot on eyes. Using liner and lamp black, add mouth, eyelashes and eyebrows. Add tiny buttermilk highlight dots to eyes.

4. Shade around entire hat and both mittens with Napa red. Dry-brush spice pink highlights on hat and mittens. Using liner brush, add buttermilk stripes to hat; add stripes to mittens with admiral blue. Highlight blue stripes in middle of mittens with wisteria.

5. Shade coat with admiral blue; highlight with dry brush and wisteria. Paint button with peony pink; shade with Napa red and highlight outer edge with spice pink. Add admiral blue holes on button; highlight at tops with wisteria.

6. For design at bottom of coat, paint peony pink hearts, buttermilk stars and little rectangles of admiral blue. Shade hearts with Napa red on left edges and highlight with spice pink on right side; shade stars with admiral blue on left edges.

7. Shade scarf with Payne's grey around all edges, next to border and around knot. Paint border buttermilk, and trim next to border with wisteria. Add peony pink zigzag lines on buttermilk border; shade around border with admiral blue. Highlight trim with buttermilk.

8. Add scarf fringe, with #4 brush dipped first in admiral blue and then in buttermilk (pour a little buttermilk into a second container first to avoid contaminating colors).

9. For fur band and pompom on hat, base-coat areas with Payne's grey.

Continued on page 185

Snowman With Heart Ornament

Continued from page 175

Snowman With Heart Ornament

"Melt My Heart" Pillow

Continued from page 165

You

White Print A

Orange Print

White Print B

Red Print

White Print A

melt my Heart

"Melt My Heart" Pillow

All Snowmen Go To Heaven

Continued from page 168

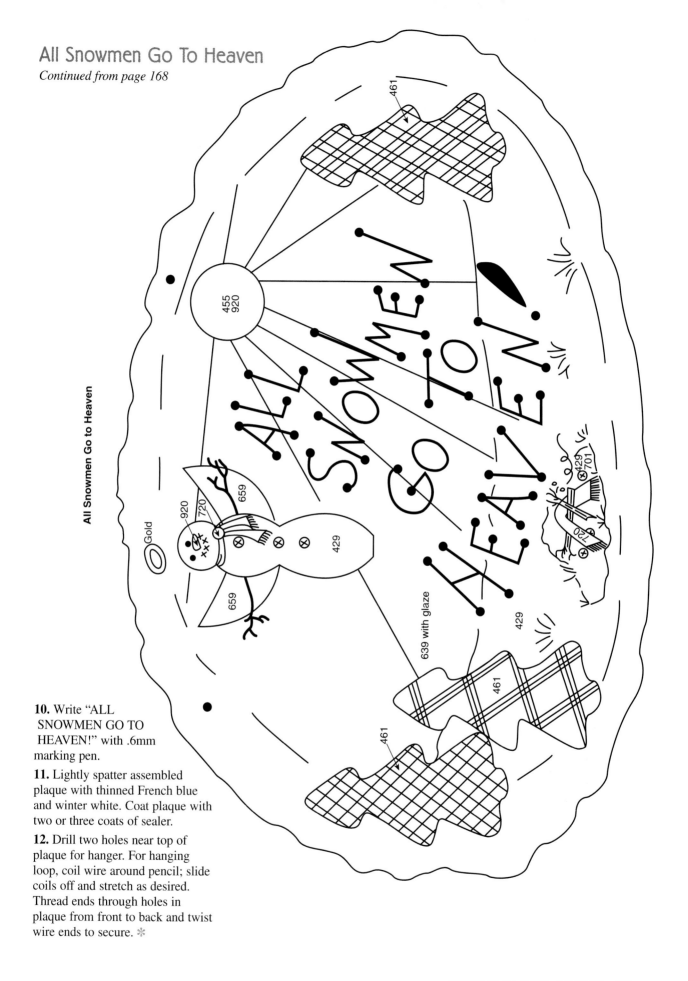

10. Write "ALL SNOWMEN GO TO HEAVEN!" with .6mm marking pen.

11. Lightly spatter assembled plaque with thinned French blue and winter white. Coat plaque with two or three coats of sealer.

12. Drill two holes near top of plaque for hanger. For hanging loop, coil wire around pencil; slide coils off and stretch as desired. Thread ends through holes in plaque from front to back and twist wire ends to secure. ✲

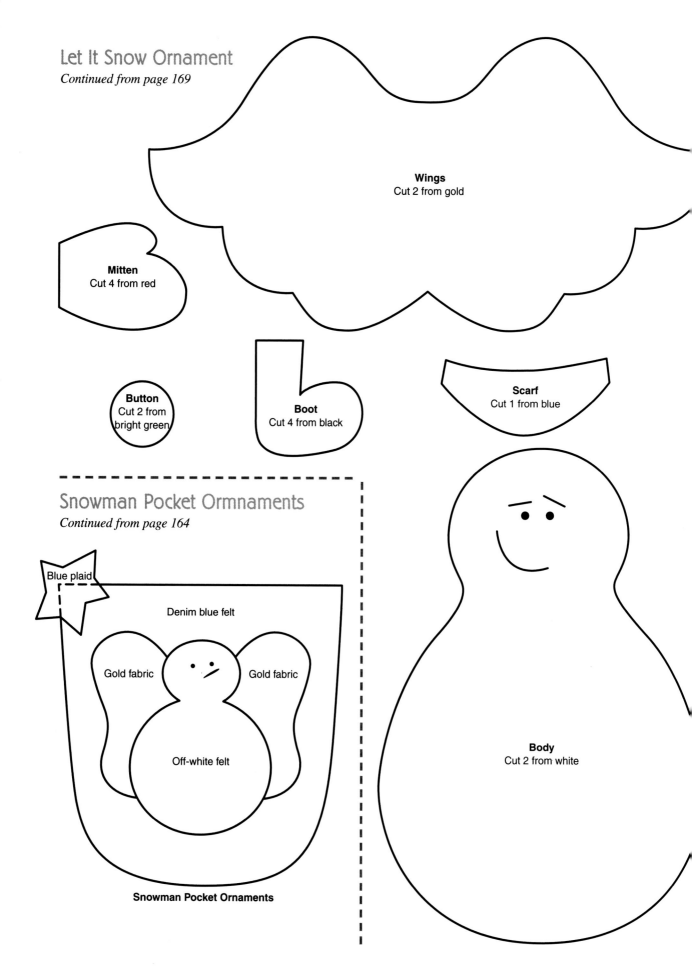

Let It Snow Ornament
Continued from page 169

Wings
Cut 2 from gold

Mitten
Cut 4 from red

Button
Cut 2 from bright green

Boot
Cut 4 from black

Scarf
Cut 1 from blue

Snowman Pocket Ormnaments
Continued from page 164

Blue plaid

Denim blue felt

Gold fabric

Gold fabric

Off-white felt

Snowman Pocket Ornaments

Body
Cut 2 from white

Snow Angel Couple

Continued from page 171

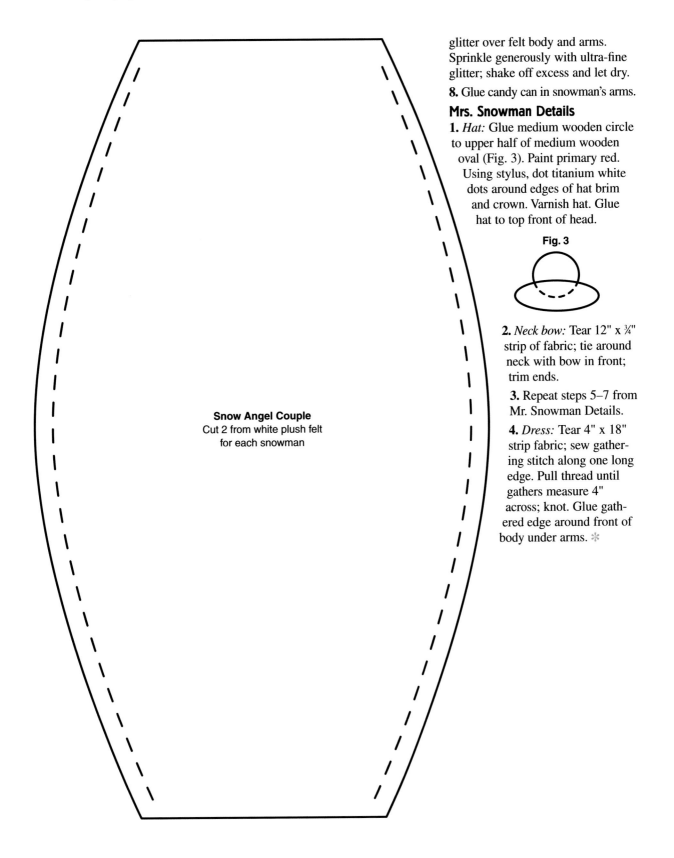

Snow Angel Couple
Cut 2 from white plush felt
for each snowman

glitter over felt body and arms. Sprinkle generously with ultra-fine glitter; shake off excess and let dry.

8. Glue candy can in snowman's arms.

Mrs. Snowman Details

1. *Hat:* Glue medium wooden circle to upper half of medium wooden oval (Fig. 3). Paint primary red. Using stylus, dot titanium white dots around edges of hat brim and crown. Varnish hat. Glue hat to top front of head.

Fig. 3

2. *Neck bow:* Tear 12" x ¾" strip of fabric; tie around neck with bow in front; trim ends.

3. Repeat steps 5–7 from Mr. Snowman Details.

4. *Dress:* Tear 4" x 18" strip fabric; sew gathering stitch along one long edge. Pull thread until gathers measure 4" across; knot. Glue gathered edge around front of body under arms. ✳

Snow Angel Pillow

Cool Christmas Door
Continued from page 178

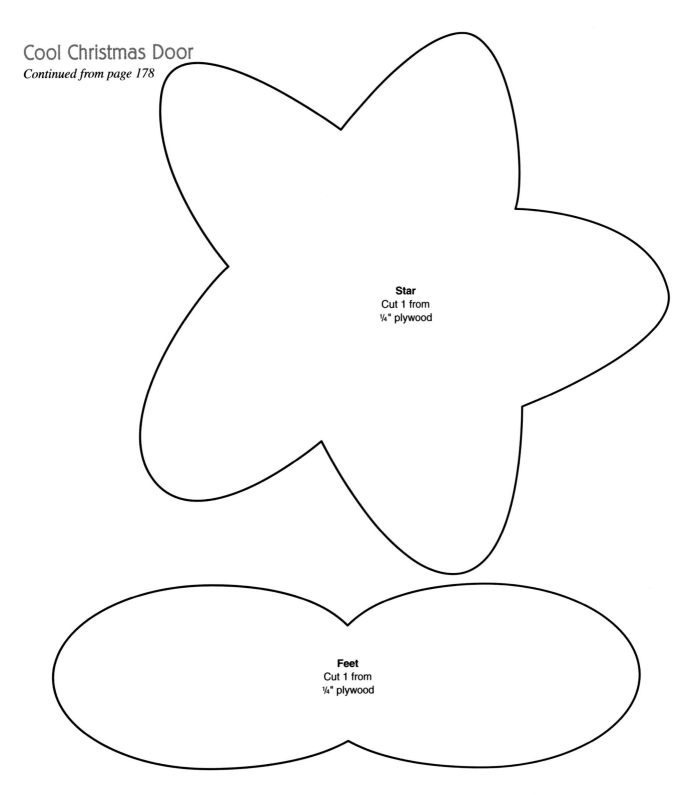

Star
Cut 1 from
¼" plywood

Feet
Cut 1 from
¼" plywood

While paint is still wet, use liner brush and buttermilk paint to pull out and define individual "hairs."

10. Paint star with another coat of buttermilk; sprinkle ultra-fine glitter over star while paint is still wet. When paint is dry, shade edges with admiral blue.

11. For sign, add lettering for "Have a cool Christmas" with admiral blue and #6 brush. Shade edges of sign with admiral blue. Paint peony pink heart as shown; shade left side with Napa red and highlight right side with spice pink.

Assembly & Finishing

1. Glue mittens to sign; glue nose, feet and sign to snowman; glue star and snowman to frame.

2. Spray entire piece with a coat or two of matte-finish varnish; let dry.

3. Attach sawtooth hanger at top center on back. ❋

Patterns continued on page 186

Mitten
Cut 2 from
¼" plywood

Nose
Cut 1 from
¼" plywood

Snowman
Enlarge by 154%
Cut 1 from ¼" plywood

Buyer's Guide

If you are unable to locate a product locally, contact the manufacturers listed below for the closest retail or mail-order source in your area.

Aleene's
Div. of Duncan Enterprises
5673 E. Shields Ave.
Fresno, CA 93727
(800) 237-2642,
www.duncan-enterprises.com

American Traditional Stencils/ Stencil Outlet
442 First New Hampshire Turnpike
Northwood, NH 03261-9754
(800) 278-3624

Amerock
4000 Auburn St.
Rockford, IL 61125-7918
(815) 969-6308
www.amerock.com
(Products are usually found in hardware stores)

API
520 Cleveland Ave.
Albany, CA 94710
(800) 776-7616
www.crafterspick.com

BagWorks Inc.
3301-C S. Cravens Rd.
Fort Worth, TX 76119
(800) 365-7423
www.bagworks.com

Beacon Adhesives/ Signature Mktg. & Mfg.
P.O. Box 427
Wyckoff, NJ 07481
(800) 865-7238
www.beacon1.com

Blumenthal Lansing Co.
1929 Main St.
Lansing, IA 52151
(800) 553-4158
www.blulans@salamander.com

Cernit
Mail-order source: **Wenzel Miniatures**
2650 Amy Place
Port Hueneme. CA 93041
(805) 984-5446
www.cernit.com

Charles Craft
P.O. Box 1049
Laurinburg, NC 28353
(910) 844-3521
e-mail: ccraft@carolina.net

Coats & Clark Inc.
Consumer Service
P.O. Box 12229
Greenville, SC 29612-0229
(800) 648-1479
www.coatsandclark.com

Cousin Corp. of America
P.O. Box 2918
Largo, FL 33779
(800) 366-2687
e-mail: custserve@enterpriseart.com

Crafts Etc.!
7717 S.W. 44th St.
Oklahoma City, OK 73179
(405) 745-1200
www.craftsetc.com

Creative Beginnings
P.O. Box 1330
Morro Bay, CA 93442
(800) 367-1739
www.creative-beginnings.com

D&CC
428 S. Zelta
Wichita, KS 67207
(800) 835-3013
e-mail: dcc@feist.com

DMC Corp.
Hackensack Avenue, Bldg. 10-A
South Kearny, NJ 07032-4688
(800) 275-4117
www.dmc-usa.com

Daler-Rowney USA
2 Corporate Dr.
Cranbury, NJ 08512-9584
(609) 655-5252

Darice Inc.
Mail-order source
Bolek's
P.O. Box 465
330 N. Tuscarawas Ave.
Dover, OH 44622
(330) 364-8878

DecoArt
P.O. Box 386
Stanford, KY 40484
(800) 367-3047
www.decoart.com

Delta Technical Coatings Inc.
2550 Pellissier Pl.
Whittier, CA 90601-1505
(800) 423-4135
www.deltacrafts.com

Duncan Enterprises
5673 E. Shields Ave.
Fresno, CA 93727
(800) 237-2642
www.duncan-enterprises.com

EK Success Ltd.
125 Entin Rd.
Clifton, NJ 07014
(800) 524-1349
www.eksuccess.com

Fibre-Craft Materials Corp.
Mail-order source: **Kirchen Brothers**
P.O. Box 1016
Skokie, IL 60076
(800) 378-5024
kirchenbro@aol.com

Fiskars Inc.
7811 W. Stewart Ave.
Wausau, WI 54401
(800) 950-0203, Ext. 1277;
www.fiskars.com

Folk Art/Plaid Enterprises Inc.
1649 International Ct.
Norcross, GA 30093
(800) 842-4197
www.plaidonline.com

Forster Inc./Diamond Brands
1800 Cloquet Ave.
Cloquet, MN 55720
(218) 879-6700
www.diamondbrands.com

Gareosol/Gare Inc.
165 Rosemont St.
Haverhill, MA 01831
(978) 373-9131
www.information@gare.com

Jesse James & Co.
615 N. New St.
Allentown, PA 18102
(610) 435-7899; www.dressitup.com

Kreinik Mfg. Co. Inc.
3106 Timanus Ln., #101
Baltimore, MD 21244-2871
(800) 537-2166; www.kreinik.com

Krylon/Sherwin-WilliamsCo
Craft Customer Service
101 Prospect N.W.
Cleveland, OH 445
(800) 247-3268

Kunin Felt Co./Foss Mftg. Co. Inc.
P.O. Box 5000
Hampton, NH 03842-5000
(800) 292-7900
www.kuninfelt.com

Lara's Crafts/Div. of Woodworks
590 N. Beach
Fort Worth, TX 76111
(800) 232-5272; www.larascrafts.com

Loew-Cornell Inc.
563 Chestnut Ave.
Teaneck, NJ 07666
(201) 836-7070; www.loew-cornell.com

Micron/Sakura of America
(800) 776-6257
express@sakuraofamerica.com

Nicole/Sbar's Inc.
14 Sbar Blvd.
Moorestown, NJ 08057
(856) 234-8220

C.M. Offray & Son/ Lion Brand Co. Inc.
Route 24
Chester, NJ 07930-0601
(908) 879-4700
www.offray.com

One & Only Creations
P.O. Box 2730
Napa, CA 94558
(800) 262-6768; www.oneandonlycreations.com

Pellon Division/
Freudenberg Nonwovens
1040 Avenue of the Americas, 14th floor
New York, NY 10018
(800) 248-5938

Plaid Enterprises Inc.
1649 International Ct.
Norcross, GA 30093
(800) 842-4197
www.plaidonline.com

Provo Craft
Mail-order source: **Creative Express**
295 W. Center St.
Provo, UT
(800) 563-8679
www.creativexpress.com

Robert Simmons Inc./ Daler-Rowney USA
2 Corporate Dr.
Cranbury, NJ 08512-9584
(609) 655-5252

Royal Brush Mfg. Inc.
6707 Broadway
Merrillville, IN 46410
(219) 660-4170

Sculpey III/Polyform Products Co.
1901 Estes
Elk Grove Village, IL 60007
(847) 427-0020
www.sculpey.com

Styrofoam/Dow Chemical Co.
Plastic Technical Support
P.O. Box 1206
Midland, MI 486441-1206
(800) 441-4369

Therm O Web
770 Glenn Ave.
Wheeling, IL 60090
(847) 520-5200
www.thermoweb.com

Tulip
Div. of Duncan Enterprises
5673 E. Shields Ave.,
Fresno, CA 93727
(800) 438-6226
www.duncan-enterprises.com

Twice as Nice Designs
2240 S.E. 72nd St.
Runnels, IA 50237
(515) 266-6535
www.twiceasnice.com

Walnut Hollow Farms Inc.
1409 St. Rd. 23
Dodgeville, WI 53533-2112
(800) 950-5101
www.walnuthollow.com

Wang's Inc.
4250 Shelby Dr.
Memphis, TN 38118
(800) 829-2647; www.wangs.com

The Warm Company
954 E. Union St.
Seattle, WA 98122
(800) 234-WARM
www.adhost.com/warmcompany/products.html

Wimpole Street Creations
Mail-order source: **Barrett House**
P.O. Box 540585
North Salt Lake, UT 84054-0585
(801) 299-0700
www.barrett-house.com

Woodworks
4521 Anderson Blvd.
Forth Worth, TX 76117
(817) 581-5230
www.woodwrks.com

Wrights
P.O. Box 398
West Warren, MA 01092
(413) 436-7732, ext. 445
www.wrights.com

Zig/EK Success Ltd.
125 Entin Rd.
Clifton, NJ 07014
(800) 524-1349
www.eksuccess.com

Zweigart/Joan Roggitt Ltd.
121 Arthur Ave.
Colonia, NJ 07067
(800) 931-4545
www.zweigart.com

General Instructions

Materials
In addition to the materials listed for each craft, some of the following crafting supplies may be needed to complete your projects. No doubt most of these are already on hand in your "treasure chest" of crafting aids. If not, you may want to gather them before you begin working so that you'll be able to complete each design quickly and without a hitch!

General Crafts
- Scissors
- Pencil
- Ruler
- Tracing paper
- Craft knife
- Heavy-duty craft cutters or wire nippers
- Plenty of newspapers to protect work surface

Painted Items
- Paper towels
- Paper or plastic foam plate or tray to use as a disposable paint palette for holding and mixing paints
- Plastic—a garbage bag, grocery sack, etc.—to protect your work surface
- Container of water or other recommended cleaning fluid for rinsing and cleaning brushes

Fabric Projects
- Iron and ironing board
- Pressing cloth
- Basic sewing notions
- Rotary cutter and self-healing mat
- Air-soluble markers
- Tailor's chalk

Needlework Designs
- Embroidery scissors
- Iron and ironing board
- Thick terry towel
- Air-soluble markers
- Tailor's chalk

Woodworking
- Rubber or latex gloves
- Safety goggles

Reproducing Patterns & Templates

The patterns provided in this book are shown right side up, as they should look on the finished project; a few oversize patterns that need to be enlarged are clearly marked. Photocopiers with enlarging capabilities are readily available at copy stores and office supply stores. Simply copy the page, setting the photocopier to enlarge the pattern to the percentage indicated.

Patterns that do not need to be enlarged may be reproduced simply by placing a piece of tracing paper or vellum over the pattern in the book, and tracing the outlines carefully with a pencil or other marker.

Once you've copied your pattern pieces, cut them out and use these pieces as templates to trace around. Secure them as needed with pins or pattern weights.

If you plan to reuse the patterns or if the patterns are more intricate, with sharp points, etc., make sturdier templates by gluing the copied page of patterns onto heavy cardboard or template plastic. Let the glue dry, then cut out the pieces with a craft knife.

Depending on the application, it may be preferable to trace the patterns onto the *wrong side* of the fabric or other material so that no lines will be visible from the front. In this case, make sure you place the *right* side of the pattern piece against the *wrong* side of the fabric, paper or other material so that the piece will face the right direction when it is cut out.

Using Transfer Paper

Some projects recommend transferring patterns to wood or another material with transfer paper. Read the manufacturer's instructions before beginning.

Lay tracing paper over the printed pattern and trace it carefully. Then place transfer paper transfer side down on wood or other material to be marked. Lay traced pattern on top. Secure layers with low-tack masking tape or tacks to keep pattern and transfer paper from shifting while you work.

Using a stylus, pen or other marking implement, retrace the pattern lines using smooth, even pressure to transfer the design onto surface.

Working With Fabrics

Read instructions carefully; take seam allowances into consideration when cutting fabrics.

If colorfastness is a concern—either with the fabric itself or with other fibers used, like thread or embroidery floss—launder fabrics first without using fabric softener. Press with an iron before using. Keep an iron and ironing board at hand to press seams and pattern pieces as you work.

Pattern markings may be transferred to fabrics with air-soluble markers or tailor's chalk. For permanent markings on fabric, use the specific pens and paints listed with each project. It is always a good idea to test the pen or marker on a scrap of fabric to check for bleeding, etc.

Painted Designs

Disposable paper or plastic foam plates, including supermarket meat trays, make good palettes for pouring and mixing paints.

The success of a painted project often depends a great deal on the care taken in the initial preparations, including sanding, applying primer and/or applying a base coat of color. Follow instructions carefully in this regard.

Take special care when painting sections adjacent to each other with different colors; allow the first color to dry so that the second will not run or mix. When adding designs atop a painted base, let the base coat dry thoroughly first.

If you will be mixing media, such as drawing with marking pens on a painted surface, test the process and your materials on scraps to make sure there will be no unsightly running or bleeding.

Keep your work surface and your tools clean. Clean brushes promptly in the manner recommended by the paint manufacturer; many acrylics can be cleaned up with soap and water, while other paints may require a solvent of some kind. Suspend your paintbrushes by their handles to dry to that the fluid drains out completely without bending the bristles.

Work in a well-ventilated area when using paints, solvents or finishes that emit fumes; read product labels thoroughly to be aware of any potential hazards and precautions.

Painting Techniques

Base-coating: Load paintbrush evenly with color by dabbing it on paint can lid, then coat surfaces with one or two smooth, solid coats of paint, letting paint dry between coats.

Dry-brushing: Dip dry, round bristle brush in paint and wipe paint off onto paper towel until brush is almost dry. Wipe brush across edges for subtle shading.

Rouging: Dip dry, round bristle brush in paint and wipe paint off onto paper towel until brush is almost completely dry and leaves no visible brush strokes. Wipe brush across area to be rouged using a circular motion.

Shading: Dip angled shader brush in water and blot lightly once on paper towel, leaving some water in brush. Dip point of brush into paint. Stroke onto palette once or twice to blend paint into water on bristles so that stroke has paint on one side gradually blending to no color on the other side.

Wooden Projects

Use extreme caution when using power equipment of any kind, and *always* wear safety goggles.

Work in a well-ventilated area when using paints, solvents or finishes that emit fumes; read product labels thoroughly to be aware of any potential hazards and precautions.

Designer Index

Technique Index